Practical
Program
Evaluation

SAGE SOURCEBOOKS FOR THE HUMAN SERVICES SERIES

Series Editors: ARMAND LAUFFER and CHARLES GARVIN

Recent Volumes in This Series

HEALTH PROMOTION AT THE COMMUNITY LEVEL
edited by NEIL BRACHT

ELDER CARE: Family Training and Support
by AMANDA SMITH BARUSCH

SOCIAL WORK PRACTICE WITH ASIAN AMERICANS
edited by SHARLENE MAEDA FURUTO, RENUKA BISWAS,
DOUGLAS K.CHUNG, KENJI MURASE, & FARIYAL ROSS-SHERIFF

FAMILY POLICIES AND FAMILY WELL-BEING:
The Role of Political Culture
by SHIRLEY L. ZIMMERMAN

FAMILY THERAPY WITH THE ELDERLY
by ELIZABETH R. NEIDHARDT & JO ANN ALLEN

EFFECTIVELY MANAGING HUMAN SERVICE ORGANIZATIONS
by RALPH BRODY

SINGLE-PARENT FAMILIES
by KRIS KISSMAN & JO ANN ALLEN

SUBSTANCE ABUSE TREATMENT: A Family Systems Perspective
edited by EDITH M. FREEMAN

SOCIAL COGNITION AND INDIVIDUAL CHANGE: Current Theory and
Counseling Guidelines
by AARON M. BROWER & PAULA S. NURIUS

UNDERSTANDING AND TREATING ADOLESCENT SUBSTANCE ABUSE
by PHILIP P. MUISENER

EFFECTIVE EMPLOYEE ASSISTANCE PROGRAMS: A Guide for EAP
Counselors and Managers
by GLORIA CUNNINGHAM

COUNSELING THE ADOLESCENT SUBSTANCE ABUSER:
School-Based Intervention and Prevention
by MARLENE MIZIKER GONET

Jeanne Pietrzak, Malia Ramler,
Tanya Renner, Lucy Ford,
and Neil Gilbert

Practical Program Evaluation

Examples from Child Abuse Prevention

SAGE SOURCEBOOKS FOR THE HUMAN SERVICES SERIES 9

SAGE PUBLICATIONS
The International Professional Publishers
Newbury Park   London   New Delhi

10-27-95

For information address:

SAGE Publications, Inc.
2455 Teller Road
Newbury Park, California 91320

SAGE Publications Ltd.
6 Bonhill Street
London EC2A 4PU
United Kingdom

SAGE Publications India Pvt. Ltd.
M-32 Market
Greater Kailash I
New Delhi 110 048 India

Printed in the United States of America

HV 713 .P73 1990

Practical program evaluatio

Library of Congress Cataloging-in-Publication Data

Practical program evaluation : examples from child abuse prevention / by Jeanne Pietrzak . . . [et al.].
    p. cm. -- (Sage sourcebooks for the human services series : v. 9)
    Includes bibliographical references.
    ISBN 0-8039-3945-5. -- ISBN 0-8039-3496-3 (pbk.)
    1. Abused children--Services for--Evaluation. 2. Child abuse--Prevention--Evaluation. I. Pietrzak, Jeanne. II. Series.
HV713.P73   1990
362.7'67'0684--dc20   89-10688
                                                        CIP

    94   15   14   13   12   11   10   9   8   7   6   5   4   3

CONTENTS

Acknowledgments   7

Introduction   9
Why Evaluation?   9
Typology of Services   10
Types of Evaluations   12
How This Book Is Organized   16

I. Program Evaluation Models

1. An Overview of Program Evaluation   21
Planning the Evaluation   22
Specifying the Evaluation Question   24
Choosing Specific Variables   24
Selecting a Research Design   25
Selecting the Study Participants   26
Choosing the Study Methodology   27
Obtaining the Data Collection Instrument   31
Collecting the Data   35
Specifying Criteria for Assessing Results   37
Analyzing the Data   38
Reporting Evaluation Findings   39

2. Input Evaluation   45
Defining the Evaluation Question   45
Selecting the Evaluation Strategy   46
Obtaining the Input Data Collection Instrument   50
Selecting Evaluative Criteria   54
Input Evaluation Case Examples   57

3. Process Evaluation   111

   Defining the Evaluation Question   111
   Locating a Process Data Collection Instrument   113
   Selecting Evaluative Criteria   113
   Process Evaluation Case Examples   117

4. Outcome Evaluation: Group Level   144

   Defining the Evaluation Question   144
   Locating an Outcome Data Collection Instrument   148
   Selecting Evaluative Criteria   148
   Group-Level Outcome Evaluation Case Examples   152

5. Outcome Evaluation: Client Level   158

   Defining the Evaluation Question   158
   Developing the Evaluation Strategy   160
   Collecting the Data   164
   Analyzing the Data   172
   Pretesting the Evaluation Method   176
   Identifying Barriers and Limitations   177
   Client Level Outcome Evaluation Case Example   180

II. Common Technical Elements of Program Evaluation

6. Research Designs   189

   Nonexperimental Designs   189
   Quasi-Experimental Designs   192
   Classic Experimental Designs   194
   Sampling Techniques   196
   Data Collection Planning   199
   Training Data Collectors   204

7. Data Collection Instruments   206

   Developing Data Collection Instruments   206
   Assessing Instrument Quality   222
   Pretesting and Revising Instruments   226

8. Analyzing the Data   231

   Meaningful Data Summaries   231
   Strategies for Interpretation and Action Guidelines   255

Appendix A:
Practical Guides for Field Evaluation Research   261

Glossary   268

References   279

About the Authors   283

ACKNOWLEDGMENTS

The initial impetus for this book came from the California State Office of Child Abuse Prevention (OCAP), which was interested in stimulating program evaluation activities among community-based services. Typically, community-based child abuse prevention agencies have limited time, money, and expertise to invest in high-powered program evaluation research. But, it was thought that by exercising a modest level of effort, these local agencies could begin systematically to examine the inputs, processes, and outcomes of their services in ways that would yield useful information. With OCAP's support, the Family Welfare Research Group (FWRG) at the School of Social Welfare, University of California, Berkeley, was engaged to develop research materials and self-evaluation models and to help a group of local agencies apply these tools and models in practice. The main objective of this project was to promote self-evaluation by interested agencies, which are usually hampered in these activities due to limited resources and a lack of experience in conducting research. This book is based on the research instruments, models, and experiences that emerged from this project.

Conducted over a period of four years, the project was a cooperative enterprise that drew on the thoughts and efforts of many members of the FWRG. The initial stage of this project was directed by Deborah Daro, under whose guidance a preliminary series of manuals was produced. Nicole LeProhn, Teresa Morris, Jeanne Pietrzak, Malia Ramler, Lucy Ford, and Tony Santangelo were among the members of the FWRG research team involved in the development and testing of evaluation models in the field. Alma Dodson compiled the annotated reference guide to self-evaluation materials. The final version of this book was written by the research team of Lucy Ford, Malia Ramler, and Tanya Renner, headed by Jeanne Pietrzak. Neil Gilbert was instrumental in developing the conceptual framework, and assisted in providing editorial support. Several drafts of the work were typed by Marilyn Berling, Sonja Munson, Susan Katzenellenbogen, and Wendy Goss.

A good deal of the effort that went into the formulation of this book was spent working with community based agencies in the field of child abuse prevention. A special thanks is owed to these agencies. They freely invested precious time and resources to examine how well they were providing services and to learn something about how they might do it a little better — expressing in this behavior the inherent link between self-evaluation and a commitment to service.

INTRODUCTION

This book is for students and professionals who are interested in the evaluation of community-based child abuse prevention programs. For the evaluator who is familiar with research design and methods, but is not an expert in child welfare, the manual provides strategies and resources, such as data collection instruments, that are specific to the field. For students of child abuse prevention and program staff, the manual provides a guide to the complex, sometimes difficult, but ultimately enriching process of program evaluation research.

WHY EVALUATION?

Professionals working with child abuse are under considerable pressure to provide a safe environment for and to help meet the immediate needs of vulnerable children. This demand for service often competes with the staff's commitment to evaluation. The need to act tends to outweigh the desire for empirical evidence of program effectiveness. But programs that fail to demonstrate their effectiveness are ultimately vulnerable to public criticism and loss of support.

Many professionals recognize the importance of demonstrating the efficiency and effectiveness of their efforts. However, there are considerable barriers to integrating evaluation into service delivery, and agencies often must struggle to overcome these barriers. In the course of these efforts they invariably ask: Why put our valuable resources into program evaluation? Answers to this question include the following:

- A well-planned effort to evaluate a program will provide crucial information for decision making. The results can identify a program's strengths as well as the weaknesses needing to be corrected.
- Funding authorities often require some analysis of the program's efficiency and effectiveness.
- Given the attention currently focused on child abuse, there are numerous ideas and theories about programs that "should work." The concerned professional needs information on the relative effectiveness of these innovative programs. A carefully implemented evaluation can move an argument from a discussion of *opinions* to a review of the *evidence*.
- Social welfare programs in general will be less vulnerable to criticisms of "throwing money" at a problem in the hope that a solution will emerge if empirical evidence that documents service impacts is available.

Many community-based agencies do not have extensive resources or expertise available for evaluation research. This book, therefore, is addressed to the types of research questions and designs that are feasible for community-based agencies and that can be done with a minimal amount of outside assistance. All agencies, no matter how small, can implement some type of systematic self-evaluation. Often, when agency staff hear the word "research" or "evaluation," they imagine a process that is very complicated. Research can be a tremendously complicated business, but it can also be seen more simply as just a way of systematically finding out what is going on. Focusing on community-based agencies, this book examines program evaluation as the systematic analysis of professional efforts.

TYPOLOGY OF SERVICES

Community-based prevention programs engage in a wide variety of activities and can be categorized according to the level of intervention. Three levels of prevention are commonly identified in the child abuse and public health fields: primary, secondary, and tertiary. The child abuse field contains various services at each of these levels of intervention. Examples used in this book illustrate different types of evaluation strategies that might be employed for services at these three levels of prevention.

Primary Child Abuse Prevention Services

Primary prevention services are those that are targeted at the general population with the objective of stopping any new occurrence of a disease or condition. Programs aimed to prevent the occurrence of child abuse and designed to reach a general audience would fall into this category. Examples of primary child abuse prevention programs are:

- a clearinghouse that develops child abuse awareness material for dissemination through the media;
- a theater group that performs plays about child abuse in community locations;
- parenting preparation and child development classes taught to the general public by the local hospital;
- a school-based program that sends educators into classrooms with curricula to teach children self-protection knowledge and skills.

Secondary Child Abuse Prevention Services

Secondary prevention programs provide services to specific high-risk groups in order to avoid the continued spread of the disease or condition. Professionals working in child abuse prevention have identified socioeconomic and intrapersonal characteristics that place families "at risk" for child abuse. Examples of secondary prevention programs serving this population are:

- a home visitor program that operates out of the county hospital and provides support to those families with new infants who have been identified as high risk by their prenatal care providers;
- a community mental health center that provides treatment to families that have child behavior problems or difficulties with managing anger;
- a developmental disability regional center that runs a special program to teach its adolescent clients about their bodies and how to recognize inappropriate sexual conduct.

Tertiary Child Abuse Prevention Services

Tertiary prevention programs provide services to the victims of a disease or condition, with the intent of minimizing its impact or negative consequences or of preventing relapse or reoccurrence. Programs that serve populations who have direct involvement with child abuse are providing tertiary prevention services. Examples are:

- a child welfare agency that provides family therapy with the goal of reuniting families in which a child has been placed in foster care;
- a therapy group for sexual assault survivors;
- a therapeutic day-care program that treats young survivors of abuse who manifest emotional and behavioral problems.

The Introductory Table lists a range of community-based services and programs associated with primary, secondary, and tertiary child abuse prevention services.

TYPES OF EVALUATIONS

A "systems evaluation", a model widely employed in the literature on program evaluation, can help program managers assess their services in three realms: (1) *inputs*, or those elements relevant to determining the suitability of a program's services, clients and staff; (2) *process*, or those elements relevant to determining the appropriateness and quality of a program's service delivery; and (3) *outcomes*, or those elements that capture the impact of services on a target population. These three types of evaluation are components of a comprehensive assessment of program performance that incorporates questions about inputs, process, and outcome. To ascertain the effectiveness of a program *and* the reasons for that effectiveness entails the simultaneous study of inputs, process, and outcome. "The quality of care cannot be fully compre-hended or successfully assured without understanding how structure influences process, and process influences outcome. No matter where one starts in this chain, one must ultimately deal with it as a whole" (Donabedian, 1978).

There are, however, circumstances in which an exclusive assessment of a program's inputs, process, or outcomes is appropriate. Sometimes it is not feasible to study all three areas due to the nature of the service, timing, and availability of resources for program evaluation. For exam-ple, measures of outcomes may be inappropriate in cases where the project has just commenced, where the clients are nearly impossible to track (e.g., hotlines), where the client is reluctant to provide accurate

Introductory Table
Range of Child Abuse Prevention Services

I. Primary Prevention
- media campaign (e.g., television documentaries)
- public service announcements
- legislative lobbying
- street theater
- child abuse councils
- child assault prevention classes
- professional education
- general parenting education in schools or around the birth of a child
- community education
- general information and referral services

II. Secondary and Tertiary Prevention Programs
- information and referral services
- respite care programs
- case management programs
- parent educational programs
- parent aides
- crisis hotlines
- client advocacy
- parent and children support groups
- counseling/therapeutic services (e.g., individual, family, couples, group)
- therapeutic day treatment programs

data, and where the outcomes can only be measured years after the service was provided. Inputs and process elements can be viewed as important in their own right, regardless of their influence on outcomes. Some programs will want to focus one or another aspect of their services because of specific problems they have encountered at their agency. Generalizations about overall program effectiveness cannot be made on the basis of these smaller assessments; programs can benefit and learn from whatever type of evaluation is most appropriate, feasible, timely and relevant for them.

Input Evaluations

Input evaluations focus on the various elements that make up child abuse prevention programs. These elements include staff, program clientele and participants, program resources, and supportive services such as transportation assistance. They constitute the "raw materials" the program brings together for the delivery of prevention services. These resources should form a cohesive system in order for the program to function smoothly. In evaluations of this type, the program inputs are identified and assessed against criteria of community needs, agency goals, best practice standards in the field, and unit cost. Input evaluations address question such as:

- How well do client characteristics reflect the agency's service goals?
- To what extent do program staff possess appropriate qualifications to deliver the services being provided?
- Is the agency situated in an area clients can easily, safely, and inexpensively get to?

When used in conjunction with process and outcome evaluations, input evaluations provide documentation of what exactly made up a successful intervention, or what might have been missing in one that was unsuccessful.

Process Evaluations

Process evaluation is an assessment of the internal dynamics and operation of a program. In contrast to the kinds of questions posed by an input evaluation, a process evaluation measures the way an agency operates and the quality of services being provided. This type of evaluation often involves scrutiny of an agency's service delivery system and the administrative arrangements that support that system. The program process is analyzed and assessed in light of criteria such as process goals, agency policies and procedures, and/or best practice standards in the field.

In a very general sense, process evaluations ask: What is being done? How well is it being done? Is it what was intended to be done? This type of evaluation might be selected if the primary questions of concern included such issues as:

* Do written policy and procedures on service delivery exist? Are these policies routinely followed?
* What is the extent to which clients are involved in the service planning process?
* What is the extent of case documentation in case records?
* Is there continuity with staff who deliver program services to a single client?
* Are services delivered efficiently and smoothly without service gaps or bottlenecks?

Used alone, a process evaluation not only assesses quality, but provides an institutional record of the program's service delivery system and can identify areas for program change. In conjunction with outcome and input evaluations, process evaluation can isolate problems and provide the necessary information for replication of effective programs.

Outcome Evaluations

Outcome evaluations address the overall impact of a program on its recipients. The underlying question that such evaluations ask is: If a given program successfully achieves its goals, how will recipients be different after receiving services? There are many reasons that agencies undertake the cost and effort of conducting outcome evaluations. Outcome evaluations can clarify communication with and enhance accountability to funders, communities, and clients. Questions about the impact of a program that can be answered by an outcome evaluation include:

* How well did the program work?
* Were the treatment goals of the clients attained at the anticipated level?
* Was it the program that caused the change in its clients?
* Is a particular service that the agency provides attaining treatment goals for its clients more frequently than another service?

In this book, two approaches to outcome studies are presented. These approaches differ with respect to the type of information to be collected. Information may be collected from clients either on an individual basis, or *client level*, or on a group basis, or *group level*. Group-level approaches involve applying one standard measuring tool to the entire client population to be evaluated. The same criteria applies to all recipients of a given program. Client-level approaches involve the development of individualized criteria for each client receiving services. The most suitable approach for evaluation of a program will depend on the type of service provided, agency goals, and the reason for the evaluation.

A group-level approach is appropriate for those types of services that can be said to have succeeded if a majority of the recipients leave the program after having achieved the same pre-determined objective (e.g., a parenting class that hopes to teach all of its members about age-appropriate expectations of children, or a counseling agency whose goal is that all clients improve their level of self-esteem).

Since group-level approaches use the same criteria to measure all clients, it is possible to make quantitative comparisons between different groups of clients. Such comparisons may be used to analyze whether the program produced changes in clients.

Client-level evaluation is possible only for those services where clients are seen regularly for some length of time. For individualized services with regular clients and where goals vary according to specific client needs, client-level strategies may be more useful than a group-level approach. In contrast, agencies doing "one-shot" types of services (e.g., educational presentations, or crisis services such as a telephone hotline) would be unable to do the type of client level evaluation presented in this text.

HOW THIS BOOK IS ORGANIZED

The purpose of this book is to facilitate program self-evaluation research so that it can be conducted with a minimum of outside technical assistance. Part I of this book features an initial presentation of the successive steps in program evaluation, before proceeding on, in subsequent chapters, to a discussion of three distinct models of evaluation discussed above: input, process, and group- or client-level outcomes. These chapters focus on those elements that distinguish input, process, and outcome models: evaluation questions, variables, instruments, and criteria. Specific references to the successive stages of evaluation will not be made outside of Chapter 1; the reader should assume that all the standard steps are being followed as a matter of course in implementing any of these types of evaluation. Part II, Common Technical Elements of Program Evaluation, presents simple information and instructions on how to perform some specialized research procedures. Topics related to choosing samples, selecting research designs, constructing data collection instruments, scheduling data collection, training data collectors, and analyzing findings are covered. An annotated guide to practical hands-on materials on self-evaluation is also provided. Throughout this book, examples and case illustrations are drawn from a wide range of child abuse prevention programs.

Part I

PROGRAM EVALUATION MODELS

Chapter 1

AN OVERVIEW OF PROGRAM EVALUATION

Program evaluation is a specific type of applied social science research. As with any research, its execution involves following a standard set of tasks or activities. These activities are present in all types of evaluation, including input, process, and outcome evaluations featured in this book. In practice, the activities do not always divide themselves into neat orderly stages. But, for purposes of presentation, they may be examined in the following order:

- Planning the Evaluation
- Specifying the Evaluation Question
- Choosing Specific Variables
- Selecting a Research Design
- Selecting the Study Participants
- Choosing the Study Methodology
- Obtaining the Data Collection Instrument
- Collecting the Data
- Specifying Criteria for Assessing Results
- Analyzing the Data
- Reporting the Evaluation Findings

PLANNING THE EVALUATION

In large part, the success of an evaluation depends on the efforts invested in the planning stage. Careful planning increases the likelihood that evaluation protocols can be carried out successfully and that the information gathered will be used in a meaningful way.

Planning to Implement the Study

The successful implementation of program evaluation depends upon several conditions in the agency being studied. In planning a study of community-based services, the researcher asks the following questions:

- Is the agency "evaluation ready"? For example, is information on its services and clients routinely gathered in a form that is easily retrievable? If not, what changes in the management information system are needed before an evaluation can begin?
- What resources are available for implementing the evaluation? That is, what are the staff and budget constraints? Given these constraints, is the scope of the planned evaluation realistic?
- What are the politics of the situation? How do key people at *every level* of the agency respond to the idea of evaluation? If there are groups opposed to the evaluation, what needs to be done to enlist their support?
- Does the agency provide multiple prevention services? If so, have clear decisions been made about which service or services are to be evaluated?
- Are mechanisms in place to recognize and reward staff who put their time and energy into the evaluation effort?

Planning for Utilization

In many ways, the extent to which evaluation findings are used determines the ultimate worth of the entire enterprise. How the evaluation findings will be utilized is not a question to be considered only after the evaluation has been completed. Wasted time and effort on evaluations that are relegated to a dusty shelf can be avoided by careful consideration *in the planning stages* to the following questions:

- Who wants the evaluation to be conducted: funding agencies, policy makers, practitioners, or community groups? Is the evaluation focused on questions of interest to the concerned parties?
- What are the overt and covert plans for utilization of the results? Does the information being gathered match the plans for utilization?
- Who is the intended audience for evaluation findings? Given this audience, how will the results be reported?
- Are there evaluation questions that must be addressed in order to meet funding requirements? Are there additional questions that staff or management would like to raise? If there are multiple questions, has a clear decision been made about which are the most important to pursue?

Consideration of these questions before initiating the evaluation process will provide a realistic framework for the endeavor. On a practical note, the planning stages should also involve some general organization of evaluation logistics. Someone, either an agency staff member or an outside research consultant, needs to be placed "in charge" of the study. This person is responsible for directing all evaluative activities. An evaluation manager might recruit key staff members, representatives of the agency board of directors, or other relevant parties to serve on an evaluation committee to consult with and share in the decision making. A common mistake in internal evaluation is assigning an extremely busy staff member the responsibility of managing the self-study without a corresponding reduction in his or her other duties. It should be recognized from the outset that a serious evaluation takes time and effort; there are a considerable number of tasks to complete along the way.

After the evaluation plan has been established, it is important to develop estimated timelines for completion of research tasks. This lends direction and focus to the effort. The time needed to complete these tasks will depend on what evaluation questions are asked, what data source and methods are used, and the amount of time devoted by staff to the evaluation. In general, input assessments will be less time consuming than process or outcome evaluations. Time should be estimated on a task-by-task basis, and the evaluation manager should keep track of staff progress, adjusting the schedule as necessary.

SPECIFYING THE EVALUATION QUESTION

Clarification of the evaluation question is the first critical task in conducting an evaluation. There are two objectives to strive for at this stage. One is to formulate research questions that sharply delineate the area of investigation. Here one might suggest that a research question well-formulated is a problem half-solved. Secondly, the evaluation question must be feasible and realistic in view of the number and type of resources (i.e., time, staff, skills, data, equipment) that are available to an agency. Resource, time, and personnel limitations preclude any single evaluation from answering all possible questions. Specifying the research question often entails difficult choices about what will and will not be studied.

In formulating the evaluation question, it is helpful to obtain input from relevant parties. There are a number of people who may be interested in the results of an evaluation. These "stakeholders" may include, for example, funders, board members, project monitors, and agency staff. Line staff are a particularly valuable source of information and ideas. Their cooperation is essential at a number of different junctures, whether in supplying data, collecting data, or implementing program changes as a result of the evaluation. Line staff will be much more willing to participate in an evaluation and be receptive to its findings if they have been involved in identifying the research question.

CHOOSING SPECIFIC VARIABLES

The evaluation question, once formulated, needs to be refined and specified in measurable terms before a strategy for studying it can be devised. The next step, therefore, is to "operationalize" the evaluation question. This simply means that the evaluation question is translated into concrete elements that can be measured or "operated on." These elements are termed "variables" because their values are expected to vary. In order to translate the abstract to the concrete, it is necessary to become increasingly specific about the focus of the question. Sometimes this process requires that the evaluator go through several successive stages of defining and specifying the evaluation question. Examples of the translation of broad or abstract evaluation questions into specific variables are found in the chapters on input, process and outcome evaluation.

In considering which variables to use, one may discover that it is not always easy to collect quantifiable data for all variables. While variables such as the number of parent education presentations per month or the number of clients with child care needs can be readily expressed in numerical terms, other variables such as staff attitudes or parenting philosophies are not so easily quantified. These variables lend themselves more appropriately to qualitative measures, such as detailed verbal descriptions, than to numerical summaries.

Qualitative data often capture the "human" side of a question in a way not possible through the use of quantitative methods alone. This type of information can provide examples of important conceptual phenomena and nuances, the full impact of which may not be conveyed solely through quantitative analysis. Also, qualitative data are useful for evaluations in which the sample sizes are too small to yield quantitative analyses of statistical significance, as we shall discuss in the next section.

The use of quantitative data, however, does have special advantages. Quantitative analysis often permits more powerful statistical comparisons across subjects for evaluations in which large enough samples are available. Through inferential statistics the evaluator can assess the significance of differences and correlations between variables; the results of this type of analysis tell us whether the research findings can be generalized to the larger population from which the study sample is drawn. Needless to say, generalizable findings will greatly enhance the utility of an evaluation.

The choice of whether to secure quantitative or qualitative data or both should be made during the selection of variables. If feasible, a combination of both types of data is desirable, as it offers more depth and scope than provided by one method or the other.

SELECTING A RESEARCH DESIGN

A research design sets forth the overall strategy for examining the evaluation question. It identifies when and from whom measurements will be taken and specifies the extent to which certain experimental controls will be used in the study. Such controls minimize contamination of the findings by extraneous factors. For example, an evaluation of a respite care program is designed to find out whether there is a decrease in stress levels among families who participate in the program.

At about the same time, a new agency opens in the community, launching a massive public outreach program on child abuse prevention. How can the evaluator be sure that any positive findings that the study might yield will be due to the respite care program and not to the new public outreach program?

Experimental controls can also address questions that have to do with other influences within the program. In a process evaluation, for instance, an agency needs to evaluate a change in the way it delivers service to a group of clients. How can the evaluator be sure that it is the change in delivery that is responsible for increased client satisfaction with the program and not that two new dynamic staff members have recently been hired?

These are the kinds of questions that need to be addressed in the study design. Since evaluation projects vary in purpose and method, the need for different controls will also vary a great deal from one research project to another. A range of specific designs is described in Chapter 6, showing how controls are introduced in different ways.

In general, the research design phase is concerned with the scheduling of measurements and the identification of the groups to be studied. While the design lays out the overall strategy for these activities, the choice of methods for collecting data and selecting the study participants reflects the research tactics.

SELECTING THE STUDY PARTICIPANTS

Once the research design has been formulated, it is time to determine precisely who will be included in the study group. During this stage of the evaluation, decisions often must be made about how to select a proportion, or sample, of the client population to participate in the study. This phase of the evaluation usually produces several questions:

- Which clients do I collect information on?
- How many clients do I have to collect information on?
- How can I possibly collect information on all of our clients? There are too many of them!
- What if we serve small groups — can we lump these groups together to evaluate our services?

• What if we offer our services at many different locations – do we have to collect information at all of those sites in order to make generalizations about our programs?

If one is able to collect data on all of the clients served by the agency, then one may be confident that the findings represent the population under study. This option, however, depends on the number of the program participants and the evaluation resources at an agency's disposal. When the total pool of subjects is very large, the evaluator will usually need to employ some sort of sampling strategy to restrict the number of participants studied. In selecting this study sample, there are two critical matters to consider and plan for: sample size and representativeness.

Most people generally are aware that small samples run the risk of producing unreliable results – values either higher or lower than those that would be found in the client population. Small samples may not sufficiently average out extreme scores and may not detect group differences when they exist. There are technical procedures, beyond the scope of this book, for estimating the appropriate sample size to achieve desired levels of precision. For a discussion of these techniques see Healey (1984) and Johnson (1988).

The other key issue to consider when specifying the sample on whom data will be collected is whether this group is representative of the larger client population, so that findings can be generalized from the smaller to the larger group. The only way to ensure that a sample is representative of a larger population is to select subjects randomly, from among the entire eligible population of clients.

There are basically two categories of samples: random and nonrandom. In a random sample, the subjects are selected in a manner that guarantees each member of the study population an equal chance of being selected. In a nonrandom sample, every member in the population does not have an equal chance of being selected. Major random and nonrandom sampling techniques are reviewed in Chapter 6.

CHOOSING THE STUDY METHODOLOGY

This phase of the evaluation entails the selection of methods to collect data. The methods most often used in the field of program evaluation include: audit, survey, direct observation, and test. A brief description of each of these methods is presented below and their important properties are summarized in Table 1.1.

Audit

An audit involves the systematic review of an agency's records, measuring its performance against a preestablished set of criteria. Audits are often required by accreditation or funding bodies, who may provide their own review forms. Generally, an audit examines the content and delivery of services as reflected in agency records. The items in an audit instrument seek to elicit existing written information on variables that can help to answer the evaluation question.

Survey

Surveys involve the administration of questions to respondents for the purpose of obtaining data on the research variables. They are particularly useful in studying programs with meager record-keeping systems. While surveys are a popular method of gathering data, it is difficult to gain a full sense of social processes in their natural settings solely through the use of this method (Babbie, 1983).

Surveys can be administered on a written questionnaire or through an interview schedule. Self-administered questionnaires are cheaper, quicker, require less staff, ensure anonymity on sensitive issues, and avoid interviewer bias. In contrast, interviews can facilitate a deeper understanding of the study topic, ensure the completion of surveys, address complex issues more effectively, and allow the interviewer to make important complementary observations.

Once a choice is made as to whether to use a written questionnaire or an interview schedule, one is faced with a further set of decisions on how to administer these instruments. Written questionnaires can be administered to respondents in person or through the mail or some combination of both, such as mailing a survey and retrieving it in person. They can be administered at the site where services are delivered or off the site. They can be administered in the presence or absence of an evaluator. Similar choices are connected with the use of interviews. One needs to decide if interviews will be done face to face or over the telephone. Telephone surveys are less costly and time-consuming than in-person interviews. Telephone interviews are generally limited to 10 to 15 minutes; few personal interviews are ever that brief. The

Table 1.1

Comparison of Research Methods

	Service Audit	Survey	Direct Observation	Testing
Definition	A review of records.	Self-report questionnaires or interviews.	Observation of clients, program staff, or services by trained observers.	Evaluation of knowledge, abilities, attitudes, etc., by use of a structured set of items that require specific responses that can be scored.
Use	To evaluate the standards of practice in a program.	To obtain client opinions, suggestions and reactions to a program.	To evaluate standards of practice in a program. To discover whether observable changes occur, presumably as an effect of having participated in the program.	To determine in an objective fashion if specified knowledge, behaviors, or attitudes, etc., are present.
Requirements	Comprehensive documentation of program activities. Appropriate instrument.	Ability to contact clients. Ability to obtain self-report from clients. Appropriate instrument.	Adequate number of observable situations. Availability of competent observers. Appropriate instrument.	Ability to contact clients. Client willingness to participate. Appropriate instrument.
Benefits	Unobtrusive. Relatively easy to do. Relatively inexpensive. Relatively quick to do. Can be done by multiple staff. Need access to records only, not clients.	Obtain direct information on attitudes, definitions, and attributions of program as cause of change in perceptions, behaviors. Relatively quick to do. Relatively inexpensive.	Unbiased nature of the method. Trained observers may detect subtle and/or unconscious changes in behavior.	Permits comparisons with norms for the general population. Eliminates (or decreases) bias in reporting. Ensures that all evaluation participants are scored in the same manner on the same items.
Drawbacks	Dependent on good, thorough documentation. Not appropriate for most outcome evaluations—only indicates that services were delivered.	Self-report is subjective. Self-report may be biased or incomplete. Does not provide objective data on the relationship between client outcome and the effect of the program.	Cannot be certain behavioral changes are due to the effects of the program. May be very time-consuming and expensive.	Instrument limitations often include: (1) lack of ability to capture spontaneous behaviors; (2) inability of respondents to take tests; (3) fear of test taking; and (4) failure to capture all relevant aspects of the topic under study. Development of instrument may be time-consuming, expensive, and difficult.

other advantage to telephone interviews is that respondents are likely to be more candid in response to sensitive questions if they are not face to face with the interviewer. One major advantage of face to face interviews is that they allow the interviewer to observe as well as to ask questions (e.g., respondent's ability to understand English, respondent's reaction to the question, and so on).

Direct Observation

This technique uses a trained observer to monitor a program's process or effects on its clientele. The observer's role is to be present at the appropriate time and place and to record what is happening in a systematic form.

In using this method, decisions must be made on what, when, and how long to observe, and how to remain as unobtrusive as possible. Observations focus on behavior, both verbal and nonverbal, and they need to be clearly identified. The primary reasons for inaccurate data from observations are related to "expectancy effects" or assumptions about how a subject should or will behave, a lack of specificity regarding the behaviors to be observed, and failure to develop clear recording procedures. The periods selected for observation should be brief, preferably no more than 30 to 60 minutes at a time. Beyond that, good reliable data from a tired observer cannot be guaranteed. Observation is appropriate only in situations where it will not disrupt the rapport, trust and confidentiality established between the staff and the participants in a program.

Testing

Testing involves the administration of a structured set of questions (or tasks) to participants in a study sample. Testing of clients is done to assess the level of knowledge or skills acquired by virtue of the program they have received. A standardized test is an instrument that has been constructed by professionals and has been analyzed in use on multiple and diverse study populations. The measure is typically accompanied by information about its purpose and interpretation, validity, reliability, administration, scoring, and norms (i.e., expected scores for nonclinical populations). The use of standardized tests allows agencies to save the time and effort that would be required to develop their own instruments, and gives them the opportunity to compare scores from their sample with the established norms.

Generally, testing requires that all evaluation participants are treated in the same manner, that is, given the same test(s) under identical circumstances (e.g., allowed the same amount of time to complete the test). In addition, all tests must be scored using the same criteria.

OBTAINING THE DATA COLLECTION INSTRUMENT

A data collection instrument is a measuring device used to gather information. This device obviously must correspond to the type of evaluation methodology previously selected. Surveys call for self-administered questionnaires or interview schedules. Observation of the program's process requires systematic checklists or data entry grids. An audit of the program's service delivery system requires the type of form on which one enters data from agency records.

There are three basic approaches to obtaining a data collection instrument. Each has its advantages and disadvantages:

- Use standardized or published instrument as is.
- Modify an existing instrument.
- Develop a new data collection instrument.

In selecting a data collection instrument, consideration should be given to the conditions surrounding its use in the agency being studied. Two factors that should be contemplated are the operating conditions under which the instrument will be used (e.g., time, space, obtrusiveness) and the respondent's characteristics (e.g., literacy, language proficiency). An awareness of these factors will streamline the search for a suitable instrument.

Use Standardized Instrument

A standardized instrument is a measuring device that has undergone development, testing, research, and revision by social scientists. The use of a standardized instrument is generally advisable if one can be located that will measure the variables relevant to the evaluator's research interests. There are several advantages in using standardized instruments, including the following:

- For many tests and surveys, the time, energy, and expense of constructing an adequate instrument will greatly exceed the resources available for the task.
- Test construction (and construction of some surveys, as well) frequently requires specialized knowledge and expertise.
- Standardized tests usually provide normative data, that is, data compiled from testing different populations extensively and recording the group scores. This process yields established norms for a variety of populations and thus provides a valuable criterion for evaluating test results.

There are several sources for locating an appropriate instrument. Among published works, various compendia of standardized measures have been produced that summarize different aspects of many instruments (e.g., purpose and interpretation of the instrument, validity and reliability ratings, administration, scoring, and norms). These works include:

- *A Report of the National Conference on Client Outcome Monitoring Procedures for Social Services.* (American Public Welfare Association, 1980)
- *Sociological Measurement: An Inventory of Scales and Indices* (Bonjean, Hill, & McLemore, 1967)
- *The Sixth Mental Measurements Yearbook* (Buros, 1965)
- *Tests in Print* (Buros, 1961)
- *Measures for Psychological Assessment: A Guide to 3,000 Original Resources and Their Applications* (Chun, Cobb, & French, Jr., 1975)
- *Final Report: The Assessment of Client/Parent Outcome Techniques for Use in Mental Health Programs* (Ciarlo, Edwards, Kiresuk, Newman, & Brown, 1981)
- "Outcome Measurement Instruments for Use in Mental Health Program Evaluation" (Hargreaves, McIntyre, Attkisson, & Siegel, 1975)
- *Behavioral Assessment* (Haynes, & Wilson, 1979)
- *Tests and Measurements in Child Development: Handbook II (Vol.I)* (Johnson, 1976)
- *Outcome Measures for Child Welfare Services: Theory and Applications* (Magura, & Moses, 1986)
- *Monitoring the Outcomes of Social Services, Vol. II: A Review of Past Research and Test Activities* (Millar, Hatry, & Koss, 1977)
- *Mirrors for Behavior: An Anthology of Classroom Observation Instruments* (Simon, & Boyer, 1974)

- *Family Measurement Techniques: Abstracts of Published Instruments, 1935-1974. Revised Edition* (Straus, & Brown, 1978)
- *Handbook of Psychiatric Rating Scales. Second Edition* (U.S. Department of Health, Education, and Welfare, National Institute of Mental Health, 1973)
- *Socioemotional Measures for Preschool and Kindergarten Children* (Walker, 1973)

The alternative to using published guides is to contact institutions that may have access to or knowledge of materials specific to the focus and needs of the evaluation. These institutions include:

- United Way of America
  701 North Fairfax Street
  Alexandria, Virginia 22314-2045
  (703) 836-7100
- Clearinghouse on Child Abuse and Neglect Information
  P.O. Box 1182
  Washington, D.C. 20013
  (301) 251-5157
- Project Share
  National Clearinghouse for Improving the Management of Human Services
  P.O. Box 2309
  Rockville, Maryland 20852
  (301) 251-5000
- ERIC Clearinghouse on Early Childhood Education
  Research Relating to Children
  1111 Kenyen Road
  Urbana, Illinois
  (217) 328-3870
- The Psychological Testing Library of a local university
- Reference librarians at local universities — either general or departmental libraries
- Research faculty members of local university departments such as Psychology, Sociology, or Social Welfare

Standardized outcome measures are much more common than standardized input or process instruments. Questions and concerns are often raised by service providers who would like to use a standardized measure but are uneasy about the legality of using someone else's work.

It is a common practice to borrow and build on the products of other people's research in the social sciences. This can be done with complete freedom unless the materials have been copyrighted or the author requests that an unpublished draft or report not be cited without permission. If the materials are copyrighted, there are at least two legal options.

- Write to the author or publishing company to request permission to use the materials. Some authors are academicians who may share materials free of charge. Some publishing companies offer a discount to nonprofit agencies who wish to order materials.
- The instrument may be modified (e.g., paraphrasing questions, deleting or adding items). The drawback with this approach is that the reliability of the former instrument cannot be assumed for the modified instrument. This option is addressed below.

Modify Existing Instrument

Often an existing instrument does not measure exactly all of the variables of interest in a particular study. With some modification, however, the instrument may be quite useful. If none of the available measures meets the needs of the study, one solution is to combine parts of two or more instruments and to add some original items. Refinement of the modified instrument usually involves reformatting, since items from different measures probably will not be consistent in format (e.g., some of the items may be worded differently, they may have different response categories, and so on). The items and responses should be modified so that they are consistent. Rating scales and Yes/No or True/False response categories should be adjusted where necessary so that respondents will not be confused by too many different formats.

It is important to bear in mind that the results from this new instrument will not necessarily be comparable to results from the original instrument. This means that normative data and reliability and validity ratings that pertained to the original standardized instrument cannot be assumed to be valid for the modified instrument. On the other hand, the new instrument will have a degree of face validity. That is, when an instrument has been modified in order to measure a specific set of variables, the act of modification implies a sharpening of the instrument to focus it on what it is supposed to measure. If a standardized instrument is modified, it is highly recommended that at least the reliability of the new instrument be tested. The appropriate tests for reliability are presented in Chapter 8.

Develop a New Data Collection Instrument

Although developing a new data collection instrument is costly and time-consuming, at times it is simply unavoidable. This situation arises particularly when evaluations focus on programs with highly specialized services and distinctive client populations. Consider, for example, a secondary child abuse prevention program serving families of children with developmental disabilities who are also at risk of abuse and neglect. The families have open cases both at the county Developmental Disability Center, in which the program is housed, and at the county Department of Social Services. In an attempt to foster interagency coordination between these two treatment agencies, interagency protocols were drafted to guide their joint efforts. In order to evaluate compliance with the coordination protocols, an audit instrument must be constructed to collect data related to these documents.

COLLECTING THE DATA

Prior to gathering data it is important to have a plan that takes into account the evaluation deadline and the who, what, where, and when involved in the data collection process. A successful data collection effort requires appropriate budgeting of time and staff resources. Scheduling the evaluation entails establishing an overall time frame for this phase of the evaluation and identifying times and locations and staff for the data collection. Specific procedures on how to schedule and chart the data collection effort are covered in Chapter 6.

In selecting and training those who will gather information for the study, an evaluation manager must initially decide whether to opt for a professional data collector or a nonprofessional. A professional data collector is not always essential to conduct a self-evaluation of community-based projects. Nonprofessional data collectors can be recruited from within or outside the agency engaged in the evaluation. They can be drawn from the ranks of program staff, program administrators, staff of the umbrella organization, board members, student interns, unaffiliated college students, or lay persons from the community. There are a number of factors to consider in deciding who would be appropriate as data collectors for any given evaluation. These factors include the availability of funds to hire outside staff, the flexibility of in-house staff schedules to accommodate data collection tasks, the skills required to conduct these tasks, potential sources of bias among data collectors affiliated with the agency, and the degree of commitment needed to complete the work.

In contemplating the factors involved in the selection of data collectors, an evaluation manager will consider the advantages and limitations that various types of individuals bring to the task. For instance, board members and lay persons cannot be expected to perform long, arduous, ongoing data collection activities. Student interns are placed in the unenviable position of evaluating the organization that is offering them professional training. Unaffiliated college students may not have the deep interest or commitment to ensure quality data collection over a prolonged period. Staff may be invested with having the evaluation produce positive results.

Once the data collection has begun, its results should be periodically monitored. This is necessary for a couple of reasons. Sometimes misunderstandings on the part of data collectors are not evident early in a study and take a while to surface. Evaluation projects may wander off course due to staff resistance or indifference and a change in the program priorities. Data should be monitored for both quality and quantity. In monitoring quality, it is necessary to determine if data are being collected as planned, if there are any unanticipated or unusual findings, and if there are any violations of confidentiality.

In monitoring data quantity, the evaluation manager seeks to document both client attrition and returns. To monitor client attrition, Austin et al. (1982) suggested that forms be developed that would, for instance, indicate the number of subjects to be seen, the number lost to the study for particular reasons, the number interviewed, and the number carried forward to the next week. These numbers can be followed from week to week to detect any undesirable trends. If a particular source of attrition surfaces repeatedly, steps should be taken to correct it. In monitoring returns, Babbie (1983) suggested that a careful recording should be made through the use of a return rate graph. It is advisable to devise a plan for monitoring the data quantity and quality information being gathered before the data collection process begins. Questions to consider when designing such a plan include the following:

- Who should monitor data quantity and quality?
- How should the data collection be monitored?
- When and how often should the data collection be monitored?
- What prompt could be instituted to remind the monitor to look at the data?

SPECIFYING CRITERIA FOR ASSESSING RESULTS

"Basic to scientific evidence is the process of comparison, of recording differences, or of contrast. Any appearance of absolute knowledge, or intrinsic knowledge about singular isolated objects is found to be illusory upon analysis. Securing scientific evidence involves making at least one comparison" (Campbell & Stanley, 1963). An assessment of the adequacy of a program's inputs, process, or outcomes requires designation of both the type of criterion to which the results of the evaluation will be compared and the designation of an acceptable level or standard of success.

The selection of evaluation criteria is related to the type of evaluation model (i.e., input, process, and outcome) and the corresponding methodology. So, for example, input assessments are often compared against standards of best practice, community needs, program goals, and unit cost. Process assessments are often compared to standards of best practice, agency policies and procedures, agency process goals, and client satisfaction. Outcome results are often compared to test scores, normative test data, and other a priori minimum standards of performance based on agency standards, funding source standards, or best practice standards in the field. The list of criteria identified in this book is not comprehensive. There are, without a doubt, other types of measures for programs. Perhaps it is a set of standards developed by an agency's staff in a peer review process. Readers should not be restricted by the options listed here.

It is possible to use more than one standard of comparison, where appropriate. So, for instance, best practice standards *and* written agency policies are appropriate criteria to use with an audit instrument. The deciding factor in the use of more than one criteria is the relevance of multiple sources of comparison combined with the amount of resources (i.e., staff, data, time) an agency has available for the evaluation.

Another task to contend with in assessing results involves the a priori specification of the overall standard of success. Suppose that clients were tested for knowledge of program content after completing a parent education program. The average test score for the clients was 150. What does "150" mean? Without some criterion for comparison, the "150" is meaningless. Even if the score is converted to a percentage, say 150/200 = 75%, is 75% a high enough score to indicate effectiveness of the program? Why? In order to answer these kinds of questions, the evaluator must specify clearly and concretely what scores will indicate success, failure, and problem areas in the program, and why.

The kinds of questions to consider when specifying standards against which to judge the findings include: What are the likely results? How will the meaning of the results be determined? What are the desired results? What are the criteria used to define the results as "desirable"? A simple little exercise may help to elicit the necessary responses. First, fabricate some positive and some negative results to your evaluation research question. Next, in considering the significance of these results, ask the following questions: At what level of research results will I consider my program to be highly effective? adequate? inadequate? Conducting this exercise at this time will assist in interpreting the data farther down the road.

ANALYZING THE DATA

The data collected may be classified as either *qualitative* or *quantitative*. Qualitative data are definitions, written documents, descriptions of events, behaviors, and so on. Quantitative data are numbers (e.g., test scores, number of yes answers to a given question on a survey, number of times a client was observed to engage in a specified behavior during a service session, number of staff hours allotted to a given service during the week).

Often, evaluation research will involve both forms of information. An input evaluation, for example, in which an audit is conducted to compare agency goals and objectives to best practice standards in the field, may obtain both qualitative data in the form of descriptions of any discrepancies found and quantitative data in the form of numbers of correspondences or points of agreement between the standards and the agency policies. Surveys and observations also frequently contain both qualitative data (e.g., open-ended comments or questions) and quantitative data (e.g., ratings and other forced-choice responses, frequencies of responses or behaviors).

Qualitative and quantitative data are analyzed differently. Therefore, when both types of information are present in the data, they must be sorted into different data sets so that separate analyses can be carried out. This is a fairly straightforward procedure. For example, if responses to both open-ended and forced-choice questions constitute the data, the open-ended responses would be analyzed qualitatively, and the forced-choice questions would be analyzed using quantitative techniques. The techniques for analyzing and interpreting qualitative and quantitative data appear in Chapter 8.

REPORTING THE EVALUATION FINDINGS

Once the findings of the study have been analyzed and interpreted, they are incorporated into a report that informs interested parties about the research. Often, upon conclusion of an evaluation, with impending deadlines drawing near, the quality of the evaluation report is compromised. This is a costly mistake. A sloppy, hasty, or incomplete job of reporting reduces the impact of the research effort no matter how well it has been designed and executed up to this point. There are three types of activities that are dealt with at this stage: defining the audience of the evaluation report, selecting dissemination strategies, and writing the report.

Recipients of the Evaluation Report

In order to effectively report the findings of an evaluation, it is necessary to define clearly *who* the audience is and *why* the audience is interested in the report. Critical questions regarding reporting strategies, report formats, and so on, cannot be answered until the audience, their information needs, their orientation, and their relationship with the program have been specified.

There are numerous potential audiences for a report of a program's self-evaluation findings. The most common ones for child abuse prevention agencies include staff members, agency administrators, boards of directors, funding sources, colleagues, clients, client representatives, and the general public. For each of these audiences, the style, language, timing, content, and scope of the report may vary dramatically. "People making the presentations have to be able to translate their idioms into the language that's most understandable to the different audiences" (Patton, 1986). Styles of reporting may vary, depending on the audience. For example, a report of the evaluation findings to the agency's clients might be a brief paragraph about the overall results of the study. Evaluation reports to program staff, on the other hand, may be periodic and be presented in such a way as to involve the staff in the analysis and/or interpretation of the findings.

Variability in evaluation reporting is largely a function of perceived differences in information needs and utilization of the findings by diverse groups of stakeholders. For example, if the purpose of reporting the findings to parents of clients is to allay fears and misunderstandings about the program, an informal verbal presentation that briefly summarizes the research findings and focuses more on the effects of the program may be a desirable approach. On the other hand, such a report would be inadequate if the audience were colleagues and the purpose of the report were to permit others to replicate the program. Some of the more common reasons for reporting to a given audience are presented in Table 1.2.

Dissemination Strategies

The common principle guiding all reporting of evaluation findings is that it should facilitate the utilization of those findings. Typically, one thinks of the process of reporting findings as the writing and distribution of the formal report.

Indeed, most studies will include a formal written report, and we will discuss the components of such a report on the following pages, but it is important to remember that this is only one of many possible dissemination strategies. The techniques for presentation of evaluation information bear serious consideration as the reporting style influences evaluator credibility (Thompson, Brown, & Furgason, 1981). Some common dissemination techniques are:

- Verbal presentations of the findings, complete with graphics, charts, and displays for use in the reporting sessions. Visual aids can simplify and enliven the presentation of data.
- A carefully worded press release for distribution to the media. A press conference could be held in conjunction with the press release.
- An account of the findings in newsletters that are sent to professional colleagues, community members, clients, and so on.

Table 1.2
Potential Reporting Audiences

Audience	Reasons for Reporting
Staff Members	Staff can use the information to better understand the program, how it works and why, to improve program implementation, and to participate more effectively in program development. Results can be used to enhance mutual cooperation, support, and understanding among staff members.
Administrators/ Board of Directors	Agency can justify and clarify expenditures, policies, and procedures, demonstrate responsiveness and flexibility, and provide information necessary for making policy decisions.
Funding Sources	Agency can demonstrate, verify, and justify need for the program and agency activities. Results can reveal the merits of the program and suggest necessary changes.
Colleagues	Program staff can share information with others in the field who can benefit from it and use it to improve their own programs or design new programs.
Client/Client Representatives	Agency can use results to clarify program goals and objectives or to explain any changes in the program. Report can demonstrate that the agency is responsive to client needs and is making every effort to provide quality service. Report can induce increased client cooperation, understanding, and involvement in the program.

- Executive summaries of the final report to be sent to specific audiences and stakeholder groups. (Executive summaries are more likely to be read than lengthy reports.)
- A forum, perhaps a conference or seminar, for the discussion of opposing points of view if there is controversy surrounding the findings.
- Informal reporting mechanisms (i.e., discussion in hallways, over coffee, on the telephone, and so on).
- A brief fact sheet summarizing key findings and recommendations for distribution to stakeholders.

The reporting format chosen will depend on the nature of the findings and on the audience. The aim is to be both creative and strategic in facilitating the understanding and use of the information (Patton, 1986). A good reporting strategy will be one that takes into account several important criteria. First, it will provide enough information to enhance credibility and provide a foundation for the findings, yet remain simple enough for clarity.

Of course, reports must be honest. Most evaluations yield a mix of positive and negative findings that should be balanced, as appropriate. If negative findings are concealed and positive ones overemphasized, the credibility of the evaluator, and therefore the utility of the information, will suffer. In this vein, it is important to distinguish among analysis, interpretation, and recommendation. While offering support for the interpretation and recommendations offered, there are, in fact, multiple interpretations of any given data.

Writing the Report

All evaluation reports should be made available in written form regardless of the use of other forms of communication. Evaluation reports can be issued at various times and in various ways, depending on arrangements struck with the sponsors of the evaluation, but it is common to prepare at least one final report at the conclusion of the study.

Certain key elements should be included in the final report. Before considering the specifics of each of these components, several general guidelines are important to keep in mind. First, the writer of the report should base the content of the report and the degree of explication and detail on the identity of his or her audience. In general, the report should be brief, concise, and written in clear, straightforward language that will be easily understood by the target audience.

Second, the report should clearly link the evaluation results to both the original question under study and the subsequent recommendations for action. Ideally, the form, purpose, and content of the written report should be developed in collaboration with the evaluation's stakeholders in order to increase the probability of eventual endorsement by agency staff (Patton, 1986). Before writing the final draft of the report, it is advisable to review the proposed conclusions with program administrators and staff. This practice will not only allow the evaluator to make use of their feedback in drafting the final report, but will also provide feedback to the staff about the results, so that there are no major surprises when the final report is issued (Hagedorn, Beck, Neubert, & Werlin, 1976). This is an important point since evaluation reports that take staff by surprise are likely to be met with disfavor and eventual rejection (Patton, 1986).

The task before the evaluator is to communicate in a comprehensible way, without omitting critical qualitative or quantitative substance — what was done, how it was done, and why it was done. The basic components to include in the format of the written report include the following.

Introduction

The introductory section describes the question addressed by the evaluation, why it is important, and the relevance of the question for program decision making. This section should also include a brief description of the program, as well as the theoretical rationale for its existence in the child abuse prevention field.

Method

This section explains the study's design, or exactly how the study was carried out and the rationale for choosing this method. This is where the variables of interest are identified, and an explanation is given of the data collection method, the data collection measures, and the sampling procedures that were used. The size and composition of the study sample is also described, along with an indication of the population to which one intends to generalize the findings. The data analysis plan is summarized in this section as well.

Results

This is the section in which the results of the data collection and analysis are reported. One way to demonstrate and dramatize the findings in the evaluation report is to feature a few select illustrations (i.e., charts, graphs, or tables). It is advisable not to overdo this technique as the reader might become overwhelmed and ignore them. No attempt is made at this stage of the report to interpret the findings.

Discussion

This section provides an interpretation of the results reported in the previous section. The writer's reasoned judgments come into play here as she or he attempts to explain the meaning of the findings and how they relate to the evaluation question. It is recommended that the evaluator also mention alternative explanations of the study results, in addition to the preferred interpretation, in order to provide a balanced perspective of the findings (Patton, 1986).

Conclusions and Recommendations

The final section of the report is a concise recapitulation of the preceding sections. This is the section of the report in which the evaluator states explicitly how the findings provide answers to the evaluation question of interest, and what the study's implications are for future program planning and decision making. A logical connection should be made between the empirical results and the recommendations for action. The recommendations should be described in practical, nonacademic terms, with the benefits and advantages of implementation clearly stated (Hagedorn et al., 1976). Thus, the concluding segment essentially ties together the entire report, linking the evaluation focus and questions presented in the introduction with the empirical findings, which then give way to conclusions and recommendations.

Executive Summary

Once the report has been written, it is important to draft a concise summary section, sometimes referred to as an executive summary. This brief overview outlines the main points of interest, incorporating all of the stages referred to above, minus the detail. The executive summary should be prepared carefully as it is widely disseminated to stakeholders, colleagues, and the general public. These people often have a keen interest in the evaluation or its findings, but have little time to pour over a complete report.

By following the guidelines presented here and doing a complete and effective job of reporting the findings of an internal evaluation, the staff performing the self-evaluation fulfills a major responsibility to themselves, their sponsors, and the public at large. Everyone stands to gain from this work.

Chapter 2

INPUT EVALUATION

DEFINING THE EVALUATION QUESTION

An input evaluation focuses upon the various elements that go into the operation of a child abuse prevention program. These elements include staff, program participants, program resources, and supportive services such as transportation assistance. They constitute the "raw materials" that programs bring together for the delivery of prevention services. The purpose of an input evaluation is to identify these elements and assess how well they reflect program objectives, best practice standards, and other evaluation criteria. An evaluation of inputs might consider, for example, the match between client characteristics and areas and levels of staff competence, or the "goodness of fit" between the complexity of the program's informational content and the educational level of the program participants.

Among the many other issues that can be addressed in an input evaluation, one might consider how closely the demographic characteristics of program recipients reflect the characteristics of its target population as stated in the program's goals and objectives. Or one might consider how well client and provider characteristics complement each other for the delivery of culturally-sensitive services. Another area of focus involves whether the availability of supplemental services, such as child care or transportation assistance, adequately meets the needs of the target population. Input evaluations also include analyses of predominant presenting problems or admitting diagnoses that may help assess the adequacy of the program's level of service or of the staff's clinical qualifications.

In primary prevention programs, an input evaluation might focus on whether the approach used for communicating information, such as the form of mass media used, is appropriate for the target audience. With regard to the indirect service components of the program, such as information and referral activities, a look at referral patterns to and from the agency can help determine whether a need exists for more outreach efforts to be directed toward a particular agency or service sector. The scope of input evaluations will depend on several factors, including the resources available to conduct the evaluation and the information needs of the evaluation stakeholders.

SELECTING THE EVALUATION STRATEGY

Specifying the Variables

In selecting variables for an evaluation of input, data are collected on those program elements most likely to yield information specifically related to the question at hand. Thus, for example, to find out if the program's staff training component is adequate to meet current staff and program needs, data will be collected on variables such as education, training and experience of the present staff, current client profiles and presenting problems, and the particulars regarding the in-service training currently in effect.

The major variables of interest in input evaluations can be roughly classified into three categories: client, staff or program factors. Client-related variables include demographic characteristics such as age, gender, ethnicity, income and employment status, family constellation, place of residence, referral source, primary presenting problem, and prior treatment history.

Staff variables relevant to an input evaluation include type and number of staff members, demographic characteristics, level and type of education, and amount of training and experience. One might also want to collect data on length of employment tenure and the extent of staff turnover.

Program variables include, in the case of primary prevention programs, the type and content of presentations, the frequency with which they are offered, and the geographic and physical accessibility of the program. Input evaluations of secondary and tertiary prevention efforts focus on program variables such as types of service modality offered, length of time the service is provided to individual clients per episode of care, and sources of referral both to and from the agency. The utilization of supportive services, such as child care, transportation assistance, and interpreting services, is another area for assessment.

Some primary prevention programs use broader interventions such as legislative lobbying or mass media education campaigns. Here, individual clients are often difficult to identify. In these cases, client, staff, and program variable categories can be translated, respectively, into program audience, program presenters, and program presentation. These classifications represent the same basic elements as those programs that have clients who can be individually identified.

Operationalizing the Variables

Once the input variables most relevant to the evaluation question are selected, the next step is to operationalize these variables. When variables are clearly defined in measurable terms, the data gathering phase of the evaluation proceeds smoothly since the researchers will know exactly what type of information to collect.

Case Example

The director of a secondary prevention program that offers counseling services to parents under stress wants to find out how well the staff's professional qualifications coincide with the clinical needs of the client population. The program evaluator identifies several variables likely to yield data that will help answer this question:

- educational background of staff members;
- prior experience of staff members; and
- presenting problems of clients.

There are several ways the program evaluator can break these variables down into measurable terms. The variable "educational background of staff members" can be summarized either numerically, in terms of years of schooling completed, or categorically, for example, (1) according to level of education (e.g., high school diploma, Associate, Bachelor's, Master's, or Doctoral degree), or (2) according to field of study (e.g. social work, psychology or rehabilitation). Similarly, the variable "prior staff experience" can be defined either as number of years of clinical experience or according to experience in different types of settings, such as psychiatric, residential, or educational environments.

In order to operationalize the variable "client presenting problem," the evaluator will need to devise categories for groupings of similar problems, such as (1) interpersonal conflict, (2) intrapersonal difficulties, or (3) cross-cultural issues; or the client could be described according to level of dysfunction. This classification scheme would entail collecting data on mandated versus voluntary referral status, number of prior Child Protective Service reports, if any, or total number of months in treatment prior to the current admission. As seen in this example, the process of operationalizing variables requires a thorough understanding of the different ways in which variables can be classified. How one classifies the variables at this point will determine how the data are to be analyzed later on.

Case Example

The administrator of a rural family respite program with several service sites is interested in assessing how accessible his program is to clients. He decides to focus on these variables: geographic location of program sites and transportation resources of each client.

To operationalize these variables, they must be redefined in more precise terms. There are several ways to describe the variable "geographic location." One could, for example, focus on the number of miles between the client's residence and the program site, or one could rate each site according to the frequency and extent of public transportation available. "Transportation resources" could be further delineated by classifying types of transportation used, or by specifying the cost to the client of each visit, both in terms of time spent in transit and the dollar amount of gasoline, tolls, or bus fares.

To further clarify the concept of operationalizing variables, Table 2.1 lists specific types of data that can be collected for a wide range of input variables.

Table 2.1
Examples of Input Variables and the Types of Data to Be Collected for Each

Variable	Examples of Data to Be Collected
Clients (direct services)	
— Demographics	— Age, sex, ethnicity, income, job status
— Numbers served	— Size of current caseloads
— Family constellation	— Size, number of extended family members
— Residence	— City, number of miles from agency, urban/rural
— Referral source	— Type of agency
	— Legal status (mandated or voluntary)
— Presenting problem	— Category or severity rating of problem
Clients (indirect services)	
— Health clinics	— Type of agency (clientele served, service provided)
— Schools	— Size of agency
— Social service agencies	— Number of requests for consultation/education received from each agency
— Civic organizations	
Program Audience	
— General public	— Demographic data
— Specific subpopulations (e.g., adults, children, families, ethnic groups)	— Estimated scope of coverage, size of audience
Staff and Program Presenters (involving authors, actors, and lobbyists)	
— Composition	— Number of professional, administrative, volunteer, clerical staff
— Demographic characteristics	— Age, sex, ethnicity, income, residency, etc.
— Education and training	— Years of education, type of degree, field of study
— Experience	— Years of experience
	— Type of setting
— Turnover	— Frequency, number, and duration of vacancies
	— Length of tenure

(continued)

Table 2.1

Examples of Input Variables and the Types of Data to Be Collected for Each
(Continued)

Variable	Examples of Data to Be Collected
Program	
— Service modalities	— Type and number
	— Number of clients served per service element
— Referral sources and linkages with other referrals	— Type, number, and frequency of service providers to and from each source
— Geographic and physical accessibility	— Availability, frequency, and cost of public transportation
	— Number of wheelchair ramps
	— Availability of parking (e.g., number of parking spaces, distance to site of service)
	— Number and location of program sites
Presentations	
— Lobbying efforts (mail, phone calls, personal visits)	— Type of product
	— Timing of delivery (time of day, day of week)
	— Length of product (number of pages/minutes)
	— Type of response expected
— Public service announcements	— Number
Adjunctive Services	
— Transportation assistance	— Type and extent of assistance offered
— Child care assistance	— Extent services are used by clients (e.g., number of clients using extended family members for child care in order to attend program)

OBTAINING THE INPUT DATA COLLECTION INSTRUMENT

The next step in conducting an input evaluation is to develop a suitable instrument with which to collect the data. Standardized measures that have already been widely tested on "normal" population groups will not be applicable to many input variables of interest. Other instruments in general use, such as those employed by United Way and similar organizations, while technically not "standardized," have been revised and fine-tuned for comprehensiveness and appropriateness to input evaluation studies. Sources for some of these instruments are listed in Table 2.2.

Another data collection instrument is the Family Welfare Research Group (FWRG) Inputs Assessment Tool. The Inputs Assessment Tool for Primary Prevention Programs and the Inputs Assessment Tool for Secondary/Tertiary Prevention Programs are presented in Appendices 2.1 and 2.2. These tools can be helpful in organizing the data collection effort as they cover a comprehensive range of inputs to child abuse prevention programs.

The tools are designed to be program-specific. That is, if an agency has several programs, a questionnaire should be completed for each program. One "program" may, however, have more than one "service." For example, a parent education program may have both in-class and at-home components, where the client comes to class one day and is visited by a parent aide another day. Both services are part of the same program, and so both would be documented on the same questionnaire. In completing this questionnaire, one should keep all program services in mind.

The Inputs Assessment Tool is divided into three sections: staff, client/participant, and program. When completing the questions, one should refer to agency and program records to ensure accuracy. As an aid to evaluating the data collected through the use of this assessment tool, the Best Practice Standards described in the next section are incorporated into the questionnaire format. The standards are listed in bold print after the question to which they apply. Space is also provided at the end of each section to total the number of standards met by the program.

The Inputs Assessment Tool is an instrument that can facilitate the systematic collection of input data on an ongoing basis. Once this procedure becomes routine, periodic input evaluation efforts can be undertaken with relative ease since the evaluator will already have the necessary information at his or her fingertips. In using this instrument the evaluator may need to modify and to tailor sections to the specific interests and needs of the program. For example, the questionnaire items dealing with program accessibility do not apply to home-based intervention programs. Similarly, items related to professional licensing or educational requirements may be irrelevant to programs that use

Table 2.2

Description of Existing Input Instruments

Title of Instrument: Perinatal Child Abuse Prevention Project Evaluation

Source: Berkeley Planning Associates
                     440 Grand Avenue
                     Oakland, California 94610-5085 (415) 465-7884

Purpose: Instrument is designed to collect baseline data on a wide array of
                     client variables.

Description: This pre-coded questionnaire, intended for completion by staff at
                     time of client intake, assesses the home environment, characteris-
                     tics of primary caretaker and child, and the presence or absence of
                     selected high-risk factors.

Title of Instrument: Agency Evaluation Manual

Source: Community Chest & Council of the Cincinnati Area
                     2400 Redding Road
                     Cincinnati, Ohio 45202 (513) 762-7100

Purpose: Designed for use either by outside evaluators or by programs con-
                     ducting self-evaluations, this tool provides guidelines with which
                     to conduct a comprehensive evaluation of agency services.

Description: The instrument consists of a series of open-ended questions that
                     focus on four areas: agency organization and structure, manage-
                     ment, service effectiveness, and financial management.

Title of Instrument: Self-Evaluation for Human Service Organizations

Source: Institute for Management Improvement of Nonprofit Organizations
                     2699 South Bayshore Drive
                     Coconut Grove, Florida 33133 (305) 854-2318

Purpose: Provides a framework by which human service program adminis-
                     trators can conduct a comprehensive analysis of their programs.

Description: The instrument consists of open-ended questions, checklists, and
                     worksheets. The tool facilitates data collection on input variables
                     such as program goals and objectives, program structure and activ-
                     ities, and characteristics of staff and clients; data useful to evalu-
                     ations of process and outcomes can also be collected with this
                     instrument.

(continued)

Table 2.2

Description of Existing Input Instruments (Continued)

Title of Instrument: Evaluating Child Abuse Prevention Programs
Sample Forms for a Perinatal Support Program

Source: National Committee for the Prevention of Child Abuse
332 South Michigan Ave., Suite 1250
Chicago, Illinois 60604 (312) 663-3520

Purpose: Collects data on client-related variables at time of intake.

Description: Questionnaires tap self-report and observer data related to client
demographics, medical history and status, and parenting behaviors
in a pre-coded, fixed-choice format.

Title of Instrument: Agency Evaluation Manual

Source: United Way of Greater Rochester
55 Saint Paul Street, Third Floor
Rochester, New York 14604 (716) 454-2770

Purpose: This document enables evaluators to acquire an overview of how
the agency plans, administers, and evaluates its services.

Description: Written in a "yes-no" format with space provided for clarifica-
tions, this tool covers program administration and evaluation practices, as well as staff and client characteristics and the degree to
which these support program mission. A unique feature is the listing of specific documents and other potential sources of data for
the questions posed.

Title of Instrument: High-Risk Signals in the Prenatal Clinic Setting

Source: University of Kansas
College of Health Sciences, Department of Nursing Services
Lawrence, Kansas 66045 (913) 864-2700

Purpose: Intended for use in a medical setting, this instrument helps to assess the extent to which parents of an unborn are at risk for future
child abuse or neglect.

Description: A checklist of high-risk indicators encompasses a range of functioning areas, including psychological, social, environmental, medical, and familial domains. Questions are presented in "yes-no"
format and may be used as a prompt for open-ended answers; as
such, the data collected may tend to be a bit subjective.

---

paraprofessionals or volunteers primarily. The ethnic categories listed may not represent the best description of the agency's target population(s).

SELECTING EVALUATIVE CRITERIA

The conceptualization and measurement of input variables provide a description of program elements. In moving from description to evaluation, one must introduce relevant criteria by which to assess the value of input components. Generally speaking, there are four types of criteria that may be employed in assessing program inputs: (1) program goals and objectives, (2) assessment of community needs, (3) standards of "Best Practice," and (4) costs per unit of service. Any one or a combination of these criteria may be used to evaluate program inputs.

Goals and Objectives

One approach to evaluating inputs addresses the question: How well do they support program goals and objectives? While this question may not apply to every input measured, it is relevant to a number of variables, including client demographics and presenting problems, types of services offered, adjunctive services, and staff training and experience. A secondary prevention program, for example, might have an objective to serve a population of children that includes those at risk of abuse, those who have been abused and neglected, and those who have suffered severe abuse. An assessment of client characteristics might reveal, however, that those served by this program consist mainly of severely abused children to the exclusion of the other targeted groups. This sort of finding would suggest either revising intake and outreach procedures to obtain a mix of clients more closely aligned to program objectives or revising program objectives to reflect new service priorities.

Goals and objectives are useful criteria for primary prevention programs, allowing them to assess variables such as audience demographics, product types, performance schedule, and presenters. For example, a public service announcement that aims to educate parents about alternatives to violent behavior during a family crisis may air at a time when network surveys indicate the extent of family viewing is low. A finding such as this would suggest either revising the message in the public service announcement, and hence the program goal, to one that educates the general public or adjusting the timing of the announcement to coincide with family viewing schedules.

To evaluate program inputs in relation to goals and objectives requires a clear and specific statement of program goals. Some child abuse prevention programs have a broad sense of mission, but have not specified their goals and objectives precisely enough to inform evaluation efforts. A set of guidelines for increasing the clarity and specificity of program goals is presented as Appendix 2.3.

Community Needs

A second approach to evaluating program inputs addresses the questions: How well do these inputs reflect an adequate response to community needs? Are the types of services the program provides already widely available in the community, or do they fill a gap in the local service network? For secondary or tertiary prevention programs, one might ask: Does the target population consist of those in the community with the greatest need for the program's services? Are program service sites located in areas that contain the heaviest concentration of potential clients? In terms of primary prevention programs, a community needs approach might consider: Is the type of information the program provides otherwise available to the community? Is the program reaching the type of audience with the least amount of knowledge in this area? The agency may be aware of community needs. Sometimes, however, this information is not readily available, in which case it may be necessary to conduct a community needs assessment.

A comprehensive needs assessment can provide a wealth of information to help evaluators make judgments about program inputs. Data generated by a needs assessment can assist program evaluators to (1) identify other potential resources available in the community, as well as the client, staff, and program characteristics of those resources, (2) identify local gaps as well as continuities of care provision, (3) detect duplications or overlaps in local services, and (4) pinpoint where a program needs to expand its consultation and education efforts in order to increase levels of cooperation and collaboration with other agencies (Hagedorn et al., 1976). In addition, it can help determine service utilization rates for various population groups. Some guidelines for conducting a community needs assessment are illustrated in Appendix 2.4.

Best Practice Standards

The third approach to the evaluation of inputs involves comparison with best practice standards. These standards are based on the accumulated knowledge in the field of child abuse prevention, and provide general guidelines for program performance. These standards represent ideal conditions. Not all of them are applicable to all programs, and most programs will probably fall short in one or more areas. Since even the experts disagree, at times, as to what constitutes the best standard of practice in a given situation, the standards presented here should be viewed as general guidelines and treated accordingly.

The best practice standards are described in Appendix 2.5 and have also been incorporated into the Inputs Assessment Tool. All of these standards do not apply to every kind of child abuse prevention program. Each standard is accompanied by one or more action guidelines. These guidelines recommend courses of action to take if the program fails to meet the standard. The standards are, in a sense, suggested policy statements.

The action guidelines are not the only alternatives. The program evaluator may discover other methods for a program to meet the standards. In addition, it may not be feasible to incorporate all of the standards into a program. Some of the standards could prove quite costly to implement; for example, opening a satellite office for those programs serving a large geographic area. While the best practice standards describe what programs should ideally aspire to, a more modest alternative may still be adequate.

Unit Cost

Another approach to assessing the adequacy of program inputs is to consider them in terms of the cost per unit of service. This cost is the current dollar value of providing one "unit" of program services. As an objective measure, the unit cost of providing services is the basic criterion of program efficiency (Hagedorn et al., 1976). Directions for calculating unit cost appear in Appendix 2.6.

INPUT EVALUATION CASE EXAMPLES

Parent Aide Program

Under this program, parents at risk of child abuse or neglect are assigned a volunteer parent aide who makes weekly home visits for up to one year. The volunteers, who are parents themselves, provide role modeling, lay counseling, parenting skills education, and social support to abusive and potentially abusive parents.

Evaluation Question

Program staff, in collaboration with the evaluation consultant, decided to focus this input evaluation on the identification of changing trends in client profiles and how these trends might be related to changes in the provision of consultation and education services to referral sources. The evaluation questions were: How have patterns of referral changed over the past two years? To what extent is this reflected in changing client profiles? Has the program's consultation and education component (C and E) been responsive to these changes?

Study Design

The relevant variables identified by the evaluation team included, for the client component, demographic data, presenting problems, and source of referral. Relevant program variables centered around the program's C and E component—which agencies the staff had contact with, and the frequency, form, and content of each contact (e.g., whether the contact was a five-minute phone call about a specific client, or a two-hour in-service training on signs of child abuse). The study sample was derived by including all clients who were admitted or referred during the first quarter of the year, as well as all clients admitted or referred during a corresponding quarter two years earlier. Data were also collected on all C and E contacts for the same time periods. The major method of data collection was through an audit of agency records such as client charts and staff activity sheets. This was supplemented by interviews with individual staff members to get a better idea of the nature of their interagency contacts.

Data Collection Instrument

The evaluation team used the Inputs Assessment Tool to collect and organize the data. A structured interview format was also developed to aid in focusing staff surveys on the specifics of their interagency contacts. The latter instrument was first pretested on a small sample of staff members, and then revised so as to tap the necessary information. The evaluator enlisted the aid of several staff to help collect the data from agency documents. She conducted all of the staff interviews herself to ensure consistency in the recording of this more qualitative data.

Data Analysis

The client data were analyzed with descriptive statistics in order to construct composite profiles. Inferential statistics were also used to compare various client characteristics to the referral source variable. The frequency of referral from each source was also analyzed according to type, frequency, and content of C and E services provided to each source.

The analysis provided a client profile of predominantly middle-class families with primary presenting problems of social isolation and intra-psychic disturbance. This profile represented a trend away from the client population of two years earlier, which had been more closely in line with the target population specified in program goals and objectives. The former clients had been poverty-level families with fewer resources, who were at greater risk of child abuse and other forms of domestic violence. Patterns of referral had also changed: Whereas two years earlier most referrals had come from child welfare agencies, current referrals were either self-referred or from private mental health providers.

An assessment of C and E activities provided a possible clue to these developments. The data revealed that recent contacts with child welfare agencies had been infrequent and had been conflictual in nature. There was also an absence of staff outreach to the local battered women's shelter during the previous few months. It also appeared that the private agencies were not aware of the criteria for making appropriate referrals.

Utilization of Findings

These findings were reported to the program director, staff, and advisory board members during a staff meeting set aside for this purpose. After a joint discussion on how to use the information, it was decided to step up C and E services to welfare agencies and the shelter, inviting these providers to exchange in-service trainings in order to improve interagency communication and cooperation. Staff also agreed on the need to meet with the private service providers to clarify referral criteria. These actions are consistent with best practice standards, which suggest educating referral sources on the services offered and the type of referrals desired.

Parent Education Program

This is a primary prevention program that provides education and referral services to first-time parents. Program participants attend a total of eight weekly classes, which address subjects such as normative child development, parenting practices, abuse prevention resources, other community resources for parents, household management, and relationship dynamics. Class sizes are small to encourage open discussion on these topics. The program is intended to serve parents of low socioeconomic status who use the perinatal services of a public hospital.

Evaluation Question

The program evaluator, together with advisory board members and teaching staff, defined the following evaluation question: How well-matched is the program approach to the characteristics of the participant population?

Study Design

In designing the evaluation, interest in the characteristics of the participant population focused on their educational levels and baseline knowledge of the curriculum. Program variables included the degree of complexity, the content, and the delivery format of the program's curriculum. This type of input design also lends itself well to use in conjunction with an outcome evaluation since the collection of data on baseline knowledge could also serve as a pretest for the latter type of study. The study sample was composed of all program participants who registered for classes during a given month and who agreed to complete assessment questionnaires. Each potential participant was approached before the date of the first session and asked to take part in an individual interview before the sessions began. Data on the program variables of interest were collected primarily by a content analysis of the curriculum guide provided by teaching staff, and supplemented by direct classroom observation.

Data Collection Instrument

The Inputs Assessment Tool was used to collect general information on participant and program curriculum components. This was supplemented by questionnaires constructed by the evaluator in collaboration with teaching staff that tapped participant knowledge of curriculum content. The data on participant characteristics were collected by the evaluator with the assistance of student interns during half-hour interviews before the start of the first session. In addition, participants completed questionnaires at the beginning of the first class to assess the extent of their baseline knowledge of the curriculum content.

Data Analysis

The data were analyzed using descriptive statistics to produce a composite profile of participant education and knowledge levels, which was then compared to curriculum characteristics. It was found that program participants and the program curriculum were somewhat mismatched in that the participants had attained an average of 13 years of education, while the curriculum was geared to only the eleventh grade level. Also, participants in general already knew about half of the curriculum content, even before the start of the first session.

Utilization of Findings

Once the evaluation findings were communicated to the teaching staff, they were able to revise the curriculum content accordingly. By using the results in this way the program was brought in line with Best Practice Standards, which specify that data on participant characteristics should be collected prior to the presentation so that the content can be tailored to the audience for which it is intended.

PROGRAM INPUTS ASSESSMENT TOOL: PRIMARY PREVENTION PROGRAMS

DIRECTIONS: Complete this questionnaire, referring to agency and program records wherever possible to ensure accuracy. Be as specific as possible, and indicate N/A next to the item if the information is not available. The questions in boxes refer to best practice standards derived from the child welfare literature. Indicate whether these standards are reflected in your program by circling Y for Yes and N for No. Space is provided to total your "Best Practice" points at the end of this questionnaire. This total, when compared to the total possible best practice points (listed on the last page) will give you an idea of how closely your program is aligned with the best practice standards. (See Chapter 2 for further clarification of how to use the best practice standards as a criterion measure.)

THE PROGRAM PARTICIPANTS ("PARTICIPANTS" AS USED IN THIS SECTION ALSO REFERS TO AUDIENCE MEMBERS.)

1. What is the estimated size of the target population?
2. What percent of the target population does the program attempt to reach annually?
3. What are the estimated population characteristics of the persons reached by your program? (Give number and percent of total population.)
   a. Rural/Urban Characteristics

	No.	%
Rural	_____	_____
Urban	_____	_____

b. Ethnicity (Number and percent of total population)

	No.	%		No.	%
White	___	___	Asian	___	___
Black	___	___	Pacific Islander	___	___
Hispanic	___	___	Other (specify:	___	___
Native American	___	___	_____)		
			Unknown	___	___

c. Primary Language Spoken (List primary languages, number and percent of population speaking each language.)

Language	No.	%
_____	___	___
_____	___	___
_____	___	___

d. Gender (List number of participants and percent of total.)

	No.	%
Female	___	___
Male	___	___

e. Marital Status of Parent/Adult (by number and percent)

	No.	%		No.	%
Never married	___	___	Divorced	___	___
Married	___	___	Separated	___	___
Widowed	___	___	Unknown	___	___

f. Pregnancy Status of Women Participants

	No.	%
Pregnant	___	___
Not Pregnant (between 12 and 46 Years)	___	___
Not of Childbearing Age	___	___

g. Employment Status of Parent/Adult

	No.	%		No.	%
Employed Full-time	___	___	Unemployed	___	___
Employed Part-time	___	___	Retired/Disabled	___	___
Seasonally Employed	___	___	Unknown	___	___

h. Area of Residence (List three most common areas of residence, number and percent residing in each locale.)

Community	No.	%
_____	___	___
_____	___	___
_____	___	___

i. Annual Family Income

	No.	%		No.	%
Less than 5,000	___	___	15,000-19,999	___	___
5,999-9,999	___	___	20,999-24,999	___	___
10,000-14,999	___	___	25,000 +	___	___

Is demographic information on the population routinely collected and aggregated? (National Center for Child Advocacy, 1976)	Y N
Does the majority of program staff have experience working with this type of program? (Peat et al., 1978)	Y N

4. a. Has the typical participant profile changed significantly in the past two years?

___ Yes

___ No

b. Since the program began?

___ Yes

___ No

c. If yes to either of the above, identify major changes in the participant population.

Characteristics at Program's Inception	Characteristics Two Years Ago	Current Characteristics
_____	_____	_____
_____	_____	_____
_____	_____	_____

5. What specific population(s) is the program mandated to serve?

Population	Mandated by Whom?
_____	_____

6. What characteristics define the program's target population (i.e., intended not actual) as delineated in the program's goals and objectives?

7. How many referrals for child abuse/neglect intervention services are received and/or requested by participants after participation in the program?

THE STAFF

1. What are the demographics of the current staff? (Include all staff members, both salaried or contracted, and volunteers)

a. Ethnicity

	No.	%		No.	%
White	___	___	Asian	___	___
Black	___	___	Pacific Islander	___	___
Hispanic	___	___	Other (specify:	___	___
Native American	___	___	_____)		

b. Languages Spoken with Proficiency Other than English

Language	No.	%
_____	___	___
_____	___	___
_____	___	___

c. Gender

	No.	%
Female	___	___
Male	___	___

Are data on staff characteristics routinely collected and
aggregated?   Y   N

Are all staff sensitive to cultural and ethnic differences
between staff and participants, and among participants?   Y   N
(Peat, Marwick, & Mitchell, 1978)

---

2. Types of Staff (List numbers and percent of total staff.)

	No.	%		No.	%
Line staff	___	___	Volunteer/Intern	___	___
Administrative	___	___	Contract	___	___

3. What are the qualifications of program staff (including paid, contract, and volunteer staff members)?

a. Educational Level

	No.	%		No.	%
High school	___	___	Master's degree	___	___
Associate degree	___	___	Doctoral degree	___	___
Bachelor's degree	___	___			

b. Field of Study

	No.	%		No.	%
Psychology	___	___	Education	___	___
Sociology	___	___	Medicine	___	___
Social work	___	___	Other (specify:	___	___
			_____)		

c. Professional Licenses

	No.	%		No.	%
LCSW	___	___	ECE Credential	___	___
RN/BSN	___	___	Teaching Credential	___	___
MFCC	___	___	Licensed Psychologist	___	___
Other (specify:	___	___			
_____)					

d. Course Work in Child Development

	No.	%		No.	%
None	___	___	3-4 courses	___	___
1-2 courses	___	___	5 or more	___	___

Are all staff knowledgeable in child development?   Y N

---

e. Extent of experience with child abuse prevention programs prior to current employment?

	No.	%		No.	%
None	___	___	3-4 years	___	___
Less than 1 year	___	___	Over 4 years	___	___
1-2 years	___	___			

Is the majority of program staff experienced in working with
this type of program, and with this type of population?   Y N
(Peat et al., 1978)

Are all staff, regardless of type of experience, aware of causal
factors and indicators of all forms of maltreatment?   Y N

---

4. Does program policy permit employing former offenders as paid or volunteer staff?

____ Yes

____ No

Are former offenders, if employed as paid or volunteer staff,
provided with close supervision by professional staff, especially during the first few months of employment?   Y N

---

5. How long have current staff been with this program?

	No.	%		No.	%
Less than 6 months	___	___	3-4 years	___	___
6 months to 1 year	___	___	5 years or more	___	___
1 to 2 years	___	___			

> Are data routinely collected and aggregated on annual staff
> turnover? (National Center for Child Advocacy, 1976)   Y N

6. If the agency uses volunteers:
   a. How are they recruited?
   b. What criteria are used for selection?
   c. Who supervises and coordinates volunteers?
   d. How often is their performance evaluated?
   e. How are volunteers oriented to the program and trained
      (e.g., length of training, by whom)?
   f. Are volunteers provided with an orientation manual that includes a clearly
      written job description?

   _____ Yes

   _____ No

> Are volunteers recruited from churches, service clubs, and char-
> itable organizations from the local community rather than from a
> distant locale? (National Center for Child Advocacy, 1976)   Y N
>
> Is one staff member responsible for coordinating volunteers?
> (National Center for Child Advocacy, 1976)   Y N

7. List all staff positions in the appropriate box. Indicate percent of time worked for
   part-time staff.

	Full Time	Part-Time	Percent Time Worked
Paid Staff			
Contract Staff			
Volunteers and Interns			

Does the program staff include the following full- or part-time positions?

Director/Coordinator	Y N
Bookkeeper/Office Manager	Y N
Program Presenters	Y N

Does the program receive input from the following?

Advisory Committee	Y N
Multidisciplinary Review Team	Y N
Researcher/Evaluator	Y N
(National Center on Child Abuse and Neglect, 1979b)	

Does the program have access to consultation from medical, psychiatric, psychological, legal, and educational resources? Y N
(National Center for Child Advocacy, 1976)

Are paraprofessionals and volunteers used for the following services?

Providing transportation	Y N
Child care	Y N
Teaching child care and home management	Y N
Providing information and referral services	Y N
Tutoring	Y N
Translating & interpreting	Y N
(National Center for Child Advocacy, 1976)	

THE PROGRAM

1. What service(s) does the program provide?
2. How many people of each target group are reached by the program each year?

a. Group Presentations to:	No. Reached	Percent of Total
Parents	_____	_____
Children	_____	_____
The Public	_____	_____
Teachers	_____	_____
b. Media Presentations		
Television	_____	_____
Radio	_____	_____
Newspapers	_____	_____
Other (specify: _____)	_____	_____

3. How many presentations are given each year in each of the following program categories?

	No. of Presentations	Percent of Total
a. Group Presentations to:		
Parents	_____	_____
Children	_____	_____
The Public	_____	_____
Teachers	_____	_____
Other Professionals/Mandated Reporters	_____	_____
b. Media Presentations		
Television	_____	_____
Radio	_____	_____
Newspapers	_____	_____
Other (specify: _____)	_____	_____

4. How many units of service were provided this year in each of the following program activities?

Program Activity	Unit Measure	No. of Units
Education and awareness outreach to community groups	Number in attendance	_____
Education and awareness outreach to professionals	Number in attendance	_____
Technical assistance and consultation to groups	Number of contacts (e.g., meetings, calls)	_____
Media activities (e.g., TV, radio, newspapers)	Number of households exposed to message	_____

5. What other agencies offer programs similar to this program?

Are program administrators aware of similar programs
offered by different agencies?   Y   N

---

6. What geographic area does the program serve?

7. Are program services available (check one):

_____ Primarily at the agency

_____ Primarily away from the agency

(Questions 8-11 are for agency-based programs only; skip to Question 12 if services are delivered away from the agency.)

8. a. Does this program operate in more than one location?

_____ Yes

_____ No

b. If yes: number of locations _____

   (Answer Questions 9-11 for each program location.)

9. Availability of public transportation to and from program:

   _____ Average daily cost of transportation (1 round trip)

   _____ Average daily round trip travel time for participants

   _____ Distance between public transit stop and program site

10. Private transportation

   a. Is parking available?

     _____ Yes

     _____ No

     If yes: Daily cost of parking   _____

           Distance to program site   _____

   b. Average distance between participant's home and program location:

     _____ miles

Are participants able to get to the program easily, inexpensively, and safely through:

   Inexpensive public transportation?   Y N

   Public bus/train stops near site?   Y N

   Minimal parking costs?   Y N

   Well-lit and patrolled parking lots and bus stops?   Y N

Are program sites located in safe neighborhoods?   Y N

---

11. What are the program's days and hours of operation?

   Days of the week   _____

   Hours of the day   _____

Is there flexibility in scheduling presentations or classes outside regular program hours, such as during evenings or weekends, in response to community needs?   Y N

---

12. What percent of groups or individual participants pay a fee?

13. Are sliding scale fees used?

   _____ No; no charge for services

   _____ No; groups charged at cost

   _____ Yes; sliding scale used (range of fees: _____)

Program Operations

14. Has the agency conducted a community-needs assessment in the past two years?

_____ Yes (date: _____)

_____ No

Are the findings from needs assessments and evaluations incorporated into the program plan or otherwise taken into account?   Y N

---

15. a. Is there a written agency policy for handling suspected cases of abuse and neglect?

    b. If so, what is the procedure?

Do staff have a contact person at Child Protective Services to
whom they can direct suspected child abuse reports?   Y N

---

16. Which of the following services does the agency offer to facilitate participation? (Check all that apply.)

_____ a. Transportation to and from program site

_____ b. Child care while attending program activities

_____ c. Meals for adults/children while attending program

_____ d. Financial reimbursement for transportation

_____ e. Financial reimbursement for child care

_____ f. Interpreters

_____ g. Toll-free phone numbers

_____ h. TTY hook-ups for deaf clients

_____ i. Other (specify: _____)

17. a. Have program services changed in the past two years (e.g., longer hours, change in site location)?

_____ Yes

_____ No

    b. Since the program's inception (date: _____)?

_____ Yes

_____ No

    c. If yes to either question, list major changes:

Service Features at Program Inception	Two Years Ago	Current Program
_____	_____	_____
_____	_____	_____

Coordination with Other Providers

18. Are staff members aware of other services available in the community that may be needed by participants?

____ Yes

____ No

Are in-service trainings held to help staff become aware of services that may be needed by participants, services available in the community, and how to obtain these services?　　Y　N

Are participants provided assistance in locating needed community resources?　　Y　N

Goals and Objectives

19. What are the program's goals?
20. What are the program's objectives?

Are the program goals in writing, and do they specify the problem to be addressed, the target population to be reached, the desired outcome, and the service delivery approach? (Austin et al., 1982)　　Y　N

Are program goals reassessed annually?　　Y　N

Does a mechanism exist for input from the community, consumers, and other agencies regarding revision of program goals and objectives? (Community Chest and Council of the Cincinatti Area, 1980)　　Y　N

Are program objectives stated in concrete, measurable terms? (Austin et al., 1982)　　Y　N

---

21. What is the program's theoretical framework?
22. What aspects of the program might hinder goal achievement?

Management Information System

23. What type of data collection system does the program use?

____ Manual

____ Computerized/automated

24. How frequently are data tabulated?
25. What types of data must be collected for monitoring requirements?
26. Are records kept on program participants?

_____ Yes

_____ No

If yes, what do they contain?

Are data collected and tabulated on a regular, systematic basis
so that time needed to complete monitoring reports is minimal?   Y   N

Physical Structure

27. Are program offices and waiting areas (check all that apply):

    _____ Adequately lit

    _____ Adequately heated/cooled

    _____ Cleaned regularly

    _____ With adequate seating/space in waiting room

28. Is there a sign with the program name and location? (Check all that apply.)

    _____ Within view of passing cars

    _____ On building directory

    _____ On office door

29. Is the program and/or agency listed in the phone book, in both the white and yellow pages?

    _____ Yes

    _____ No

30. Are program offices accessible to the physically handicapped?

    _____ Yes

    _____ No

31. Is there a waiting area or playroom for children that is equipped with toys and/or books for a variety of ages?

    _____ Yes

    _____ No

Outreach

32. How are individuals or groups referred to the program?

Source	% of Total
Mailings (to whom: _____)	_____
Advertisements (type: _____)	_____
Community outreach	_____
Past participants/word of mouth	_____
Other agencies (specify: _____)	_____

Service-Specific Questions

The following questions are specific to the type of service the program provides. Service choices are:

1. Educational Presentations
2. Perinatal Services for New Parents
3. Information and Referral Services

Educational Presentations

1. What is the maximum audience size?
2. How extensively does the program plan to cover the geographic target area?

    _____ Number of sites per 100,000 population

3. Are presentations adaptable to the following special populations? (Check all that apply.)

    _____ Hearing impaired

    _____ Visually impaired

    _____ Developmentally disabled

    _____ Physically disabled

4. Are skits, puppet shows, role plays, or other "live" aids used?

    _____ Yes

    _____ No

5. Are audiovisual aids used?

    _____ Yes

    _____ No

6. Is there an opportunity for the audience members to meet with presenters individually after the presentations?

    _____ Yes

    _____ No

7. Is there a question-and-answer period during or after the presentation?

    _____ Yes

    _____ No

8. Is informed consent obtained for all child participants?

9. If part of a school curricula, is the presentation a required course of study?

    _____ Yes

    _____ No

10. Are data about the audience gathered prior to program presentation (e.g., size, ages, languages spoken)?

    _____ Yes

    _____ No

Perinatal Services for New Parents

1. Do new parents receive information in each of the following areas?
   - _____ Normal stages of child development
   - _____ Community resources available to parents
   - _____ Routine medical services newborn and mother should get
2. Do new parents receive services at home as well as in the hospital?
   - _____ Yes
   - _____ No
3. Can program staff be contacted by parents in case of an emergency?
   - _____ Yes
   - _____ No
4. Is an assessment done on each new family at intake?
   - _____ Yes
   - _____ No
5. Is the following information collected on parents' background and environment? (Check all that apply.)
   - _____ Household composition
   - _____ Length of marriage
   - _____ Religious background
   - _____ Housing situation
   - _____ Parents' experiences during childhood
   - _____ Family stress factors
6. Is the following information collected on parents' behavior? (Check all that apply.)
   - _____ Level of parenting skill
   - _____ Degree of isolation
   - _____ Use of physical punishment
   - _____ Motivation for program participation
   - _____ Typical reaction to stress

Information and Referral Services

1. Are resource lists updated regularly, or at least semiannually?
   - _____ Yes
   - _____ No

2. Does the program provide the following types of information?
   (Check all that apply.)

   ____ Stages of normal child development

   ____ Stress reduction techniques

   ____ Indicators of abuse

   ____ Prevention techniques

   ____ Volunteer opportunities

   ____ Methods to screen potential child care providers

3. Is there a computerized data base of resources for easy access by telephone staff?

   ____ Yes

   ____ No

4. Do staff know where to refer callers for the following services? (Check all that apply.)

   ____ Parent education classes

   ____ Individual, marital, and family therapy for children and adults

   ____ Lay therapists and self-help groups

   ____ 24-hour crisis hotlines

   ____ Respite care, in-home and out-of-home

   ____ Child care; sick child care

   ____ Community education/awareness outreach

   ____ Professional education/awareness outreach

   ____ Primary prevention services for children

Does the program collect sufficient data so that the program administrator is able to answer all the questions on this assessment tool without the need to collect additional data?

Total number of "Best Practice" points for entire Inputs Assessment Instrument (out of a possible 40).

Y N

For more information on how to use the "Best Practice" standards in evaluating the data collected with this Assessment Instrument, turn to the section "Selecting Evaluative Criteria" in Chapter 2.

PROGRAM INPUTS ASSESSMENT TOOL:
Secondary And Tertiary Prevention Programs

DIRECTIONS: Complete the following questionnaire, referring to agency and program records wherever possible to ensure accuracy. Be as specific as possible, and indicate N/A next to the item if the information is not available. The questions in boxes refer to best practice standards, derived from the child welfare literature. Indicate whether these standards are reflected in your program by circling Y for Yes and N for No.

THE CLIENTS

1. Who is the primary client? (Check one.)

  _____ The child

  _____ The adult

  _____ The family

2. Are case records kept for (check one):

  _____ The individual client

  _____ The family

  _____ Both

If the program serves families, are records maintained on each
family member who is served by the program? (*Planning*, 1976)   Y N

Do client records contain the following information?

Client's name, age, sex, social security
  number, ethnicity, marital status, family size   Y N
History of abuse/neglect and/or high-risk
  indicators observed   Y N
Health and mental health status   Y N
Services client is currently receiving   Y N
Reason for referral and referral source   Y N
Staff assigned to client   Y N
Primary problems and treatment goals   Y N
Objectives that are time-limited   Y N
Emergency or routine status   Y N
(*Planning*, 1976; National Center for Child Advocacy, 1976)

3. How large is the current client population?

	No.	%
Households receiving services	___	___
Parents/adults directly served	___	___
Parents/adults indirectly served (household members who do not participate directly in services)	___	___
Children directly served	___	___
Children indirectly served	___	___
Single-parent households	___	___
Two-parent households	___	___
One parent plus other adult	___	___

4. What are the demographics of the current client population? (Give number of clients and percent of total clientele.)

a. Age

Children			Parents/Adults					
	No.	%		No.	%		No.	%
0-2	___	___	17 or less	___	___	35-39	___	___
3-5	___	___	18-19	___	___	40-49	___	___
6-8	___	___	20-24	___	___	50-59	___	___
9-11	___	___	25-29	___	___	60 +	___	___
12-14	___	___	30-34	___	___			

b. Ethnicity of Parent/Adult (Give number of clients and percent of total clientele.)

	No.	%		No.	%
White	___	___	Asian	___	___
Black	___	___	Pacific Islander	___	___
Hispanic	___	___	Other (specify:	___	___
Native American	___	___	_____)		
			Unknown	___	___

c. Ethnicity of Children (Give number of clients and percent of total clientele.)

	No.	%		No.	%
White	___	___	Asian	___	___
Black	___	___	Pacific Islander	___	___
Hispanic	___	___	Other (specify:	___	___
Native American	___	___	_____)		
			Unknown	___	___

d. Primary Language Spoken by Program Clients (List primary languages, number and percent of clients speaking each.)

	Adults		Children	
Language	No.	%	No.	%
_____	___	___	___	___
_____	___	___	___	___
_____	___	___	___	___

e. Gender (List number of clients and percent of total.)

	No.	%
Female	___	___
Male	___	___

f. Marital Status of Parent/Adult (by number and percent)

	No.	%		No.	%
Never married	___	___	Divorced	___	___
Married	___	___	Separated	___	___
Widowed	___	___	Unknown	___	___

g. Relationship of Primary Caretaker to Child

	No.	%		No.	%
Mother	___	___	Sibling	___	___
Father	___	___	Other Relative	___	___
Foster Parent	___	___	Unrelated	___	___
Stepparent	___	___	Unknown	___	___
Grandparent	___	___			

h. Highest Educational Level Attained (parent/adult)

	No.	%		No.	%
Up to 12th grade	___	___	Bachelor's degree	___	___
High school graduate	___	___	Graduate school	___	___
Community college	___	___	Unknown	___	___

i. Employment Status of Parent/Adult

	No.	%		No.	%
Employed full-time	___	___	Unemployed	___	___
Employed part-time	___	___	Retired/Disabled	___	___
Seasonally employed	___	___	Unknown	___	___

j. Area of Residence (List three most common areas of residence, number and percent residing in each locale.)

Community	No.	%
_____	___	___
_____	___	___
_____	___	___

k. Annual Family Income

	No.	%		No.	%
Less than 5,000	___	___	15,000-19,999	___	___
5,999-9,999	___	___	20,999-24,999	___	___
10,000-14,999	___	___	25,000 +	___	___

Is demographic information on clients routinely collected and
aggregated? (National Center for Child Advocacy, 1976)   Y N

Is each client formally assessed at intake?   Y N

---

5. Family stress factors at time of case opening (list number and percent of clientele affected by each factor):

	No.	%		No.	%
Financial hardship	___	___	Substance abuse	___	___
Work-related problem	___	___	Frequent moves	___	___
Household conflict	___	___	Physical health problems	___	___
Heavy child care responsibilities	___	___	Mental health problems	___	___
Migration	___	___	Difficult-to-manage child	___	___

Lack of family   Other (specify:
support   ) ____ ____
                        ____ ____ _____

No extra-familial
support system

                        ____ ____

Is the following information routinely collected on clients' behavior?

Typical reaction to stress	Y N
Normal patterns of child care	Y N
Variations in child care patterns	Y N
Parents' experiences during childhood	Y N
Stressors and typical reactions to these	Y N
Evaluation of parent-child interaction	Y N
Previous participation in treatment (*Planning*, 1976)	Y N

---

6. What types of problems do clients present at the time of admission for program services?

	No.	%
Potential physical abuse	____	____
Potential physical neglect	____	____
Current physical abuse	____	____
Current physical neglect	____	____
Potential emotional abuse or neglect	____	____
Current emotional abuse or neglect	____	____
Sexual abuse	____	____
Failure to thrive	____	____
Other (specify: _____)	____	____

7. What is the severity of the problem clients present with at the time of admission into the program?

	No.	%
No observable impact on child	____	____
Injury/damage requires no medical or psychological treatment	____	____
Injury/damage requires medical or psychological treatment	____	____
Child sustains permanent physical or emotional damage	____	____
Death of child	____	____
No impact at the current time	____	____

> Does the majority of program staff have experience working with
> this type of client population, or with this type of program?   Y N
> (Peat et al., 1978)

8. a. Has the typical client profile changed significantly in the past two years?

    _____ Yes

    _____ No

   b. Since the program began?

    _____ Yes

    _____ No

   c. If yes to either of the above, identify major changes in the client population.

Client Characteristics at Program's Inception	Client Profile Two Years Ago	Current Client Profile

9. What specific population(s) is the program mandated to serve?

Population	Mandated by Whom?

10. What characteristics define the program's target (i.e., intended not actual) population?

11. What is the estimated size of the target population?

12. What percent of the target population does the program attempt to serve?

> Are data on the demographics of the target population routinely
> collected and aggregated?   Y N

THE STAFF

1. What are the demographics of the current staff? (Include all staff members, both salaried or contracted, and volunteers.)

   a. Ethnicity

	No.	%		No.	%
White	___	___	Asian	___	___
Black	___	___	Pacific Islander	___	___
Hispanic	___	___	Other (specify: _____)	___	___
Native American	___	___	Unknown	___	___

b. Languages Spoken with Proficiency Other than English

Language	No.	%
_____	___	___
_____	___	___
_____	___	___

c. Gender

	No.	%
Female	___	___
Male	___	___

Are all staff sensitive to cultural and ethnic differences
between staff and clients, and among clients?   Y N
(Peat et al., 1978)

---

2. Types of Staff (List numbers and percent of total staff.)

	No.	%		No.	%
Line staff	___	___	Volunteer/Intern	___	___
Administrative	___	___	Contract	___	___

For Crisis Nursery programs, are at least two staff members on duty between 7:00 a.m. and 10:00 p.m., with the
child-staff ratio never exceeding four to one?   Y N

Are client-staff ratios for other programs within legal
requirements for those services at all times?   Y N
(Beezley, 1978)

---

3. What are the qualifications of program staff (including paid, contract, and volunteer staff members)?

   a. Educational Level

	No.	%		No.	%
High school	___	___	Master's degree	___	___
Associate degree	___	___	Doctoral degree	___	___
Bachelor's degree	___	___			

   b. Field of Study

	No.	%		No.	%
Psychology	___	___	Education	___	___
Sociology	___	___	Medicine	___	___
Social work	___	___	Other (specify:	___	___
			_____)		

c. Professional Licenses

	No.	%		No.	%
LCSW	___	___	ECE Credential	___	___
RN/BSN	___	___	Teaching Credential	___	___
MFCC	___	___	Licensed Psychologist	___	___
Other (specify: _____)	___	___			

d. Course work in Child Development

	No.	%		No.	%
None	___	___	3-4 courses	___	___
1-2 courses	___	___	5 or more	___	___

Are all staff knowledgeable in child development?   Y N

---

e. Extent of experience with client population prior to current employment?

	No.	%		No.	%
None	___	___	3-4 years	___	___
Less than 1 year	___	___	Over 4 years	___	___
1-2 years	___	___			

f. Type(s) of clients staff have experience working with?

High-risk parents	___	___	Infants	___	___
Abusive parents	___	___	Preschoolers	___	___
Voluntary clients	___	___	School age	___	___
Involuntary clients	___	___	Adolescent	___	___

g. Other special populations staff have experience with?

Substance abusers	___	___	Developmentally disabled	___	___
Psychiatric	___	___	Other (specify: _____)	___	___

Do child care workers in Crisis Nurseries meet the following requirements? (Beezley, 1978)

At least 21 years of age   Y N

At least 2 years of full-time experience in working with young children, either as a parent, volunteer, or paid employee   Y N

Do parent aides meet the following requirements?

At least 21 years of age and a high school graduate   Y N

Are parents themselves, or have had extensive experience in the child care field   Y N

Are emotionally mature, self-directed, warm, caring, flexible, nonauthoritarian individuals   Y N
(National Center on Child Abuse and Neglect, 1979a)

Do case managers meet the following requirements?

Master's in social work or related field, or Bachelor's in social work plus experience   Y N

Specialized skill in individual, family, and group counseling, and knowledge of child development   Y N

Experience in working with multi-problem families
(National Center on Child Abuse and Neglect, 1980)   Y N

Are all staff, regardless of type of experience, aware of causal factors and indicators of all forms of maltreatment?   Y N

4. Does program policy permit employing former clients as paid or volunteer staff?

_____ Yes

_____ No

Are former clients, employed as paid or volunteer staff, provided with close supervision by professional staff, especially during the first few months of employment?   Y N

5. How long have current staff been with this program?

	No.	%		No.	%
Less than 6 months	___	___	3-4 years	___	___
6 months to 1 year	___	___	5 years or more	___	___
1 to 2 years	___	___			

Are data routinely collected and aggregated on staff characteristics and annual staff turnover? (National Center for Child Advocacy, 1976)   Y N

6. If the agency uses volunteers:

a. How are they recruited?

b. What criteria are used for selection?

c. Who supervises and coordinates volunteers? How often is their performance evaluated?

d. How are volunteers oriented to the program and trained (e.g., length of training, by whom)?

e. Are volunteers provided with an orientation manual that includes a clearly written job description?

_____ Yes

_____ No

Are volunteers recruited from churches, service clubs, and charitable organizations from the local community rather than from a distant locale? (National Center for Child Advocacy, 1976)   Y   N

---

7. List all staff positions in the appropriate box. Indicate percent of time worked for part-time staff.

	Full Time	Part-Time	Percent Time Worked
Paid Staff			
Contract Staff			
Volunteers and Interns			

Does the program staff include the following full- or part-time positions?

Director/Coordinator	Y N
Bookkeeper/Office Manager	Y N
Treatment Staff	Y N
Casework Supervisor	Y N

Does the program receive input from the following?

Advisory Committee	Y N
Multidisciplinary Review Team	Y N
Researcher/Evaluator	Y N

(National Center on Child Abuse and Neglect, 1979b)

Does the program have access to consultation from medical, psychiatric, psychological, legal, and educational resources?   Y N
(National Center for Child Advocacy, 1976)

Are paraprofessionals and volunteers used for the following services?

Providing transportation	Y N
Child care	Y N
Teaching child care and home management	Y N
Providing information and referral services	Y N
Tutoring	Y N
Translating and interpreting	Y N

(National Center for Child Advocacy, 1976)

Are parent aides used in the following situations?

Self-referred clients	Y N
Socially and psychologically isolated families	Y N
Emotionally immature parents with low self-esteem	Y N
Families under stress, with potential for abuse	Y N
New mothers in need of parenting assistance	Y N
Chronic neglect cases resulting from lack of knowledge about child care	Y N

THE PROGRAM

1. What service(s) does this program provide?
2. How long has this program been operating?
   Number of months/years: _____
3. What other programs does this agency offer?
4. What other agencies offer programs similar to this program?

Are program administrators aware of similar programs offered by different agencies?   Y N

5. What geographic area does this program serve?
6. a. Does this program operate in more than one location?

      _____ Yes

      _____ No

   b. If yes: number of locations _____
      Answer questions 7-9 for each program location.
7. Availability of public transportation to and from program:

      _____ Average daily cost of transportation (1 round trip)

      _____ Average daily round trip travel time for clients

      _____ Distance between public transit stop and program site

8. Private transportation
   a. Is parking available?

   _____ Yes

   _____ No

   If yes: Daily cost of parking   _____

   Distance to program site   _____

   b. Average distance between participant's home and program location:

   _____ miles

Are participants able to get to the program easily, inexpensively,
and safely through:
    Inexpensive public transportation?   Y N
    Public bus/train stops near site?   Y N
    Minimal parking costs?   Y N
    Well-lit and patrolled parking lots and bus stops?   Y N

Are program sites located in safe neighborhoods?   Y N

---

9. What are the program's days and hours of operation?

   Days of the week   _____

   Hours of the day   _____

Does the program provide services that are available outside of the
standard work week, such as during evening hours or on weekends, in response to community needs?   Y N

Are clients offered appointments off the site, such as at home,
work, or school?   Y N

---

10. Are clients able to contact program staff in the event of an emergency or crisis?

   _____ Yes

   _____ No

Are clients made aware of where and how to obtain crisis intervention services or referrals 24 hours a day? (National Center on   Y N
Child Abuse and Neglect, 1979c)

---

11. Are sliding scale fees used?

   _____ No; no charge for services

   _____ No; groups charged at cost

   _____ Yes; sliding scale used (range of fees: _____)

Lowest fee   ____

Highest fee   ____

12. What percent of clients pay a fee?

_____

Are all clients offered services regardless of ability to pay for
services?   Y N

Program Operations

13. Has the agency conducted a community-needs assessment in the past two years?

    ____ Yes (date: _____)

    ____ No

Are the findings from needs assessments and evaluations incorporated into the program plan or otherwise taken into account?   Y N

---

14. Does the program take primary responsibility for client case management?

    ____ Yes

    ____ No

If not, do program staff maintain at least biweekly contact with
client case managers?   Y N

Is there a written agency policy for handling suspected cases of
abuse and neglect?   Y N

Do program staff have a contact person at Child Protective Services to whom they can direct suspected child abuse reports?   Y N

Does the agency offer the following services to facilitate client
participation?

Transportation to and from program site   Y N

Child care while attending program activities   Y N

Meals for adults/children while attending program   Y N

Financial reimbursement for child care   Y N

Financial reimbursement for transportation   Y N

Interpreters   Y N

Toll-free phone numbers   Y N

TTY hook-ups for deaf clients   Y N

Other (specify: _____)   Y N

15. a. Have program services changed in the past two years (e.g., longer hours, change in site location)?

    _____ Yes

    _____ No

   b. Since the program's inception (date: _____)?

    _____ Yes

    _____ No

   c. If yes to either question, list major changes:

Service Features at Program Inception	Two Years Ago	Current Program
_____	_____	_____
_____	_____	_____
_____	_____	_____

Coordination with Other Providers

16. What are the program's primary sources of referrals? (List number of referrals and percent of total referrals.)

	No.	%		No.	%
Court-ordered	____	____	Other mandated reporters (MD, etc.)	____	____
CPS/other public agency	____	____	Other (specify: _____)	____	____
Private nonprofits	____	____	Unknown	____	____

17. How do self-referred clients learn of the program? (List number and percent of total self-referrals.)

	No.	%
Public education and awareness presentations	____	____
Mass media campaigns	____	____
Flyers and program brochures	____	____
Word of mouth	____	____
Other (specify: _____)	____	____
Unknown	____	____

Are referral sources carefully identified and educated about the program's capacity and kinds of cases it plans to or does serve? (National Center on Child Abuse and Neglect, 1979b)   Y N

18. How many clients referred to the program in the past year have received program services prior to the current admission? (List number and percent.)

	No.	%
Cases opened once prior to current admission		
Cases opened twice prior to current admission		
Cases opened three times prior to current admission		

19. How many program clients or households receive the following services, from this agency or another agency, while involved in the program?

	No.	%
Parenting/homemaking education		
Individual counseling		
Group counseling		
Substance abuse counseling		
Play therapy/child development		
Therapeutic day care		
Advocacy/advocacy follow-up		
Referral/referral follow-up		
24-hour care		
Respite care		
Self-help		
Crisis services		
Transportation		
Other (specify: _____)		

Are in-service trainings held to help staff become aware of services needed by clients, services available in the community, and how to obtain these services?   Y N

Are clients provided assistance in locating needed community resources?   Y N

Do clients receive a comprehensive service package that addresses the needs of all family members? (Daro, 1985; National Center on Child Abuse and Neglect, 1979c)   Y N

---

20. How frequently do program staff have contact with the following agencies? (Indicate for applicable agencies.)

_____ CPS

_____ Law enforcement

_____ Schools

_____ Hospitals

Do program staff function as part of a multidisciplinary team, composed of representatives of these agencies, which meets at least monthly to discuss issues of child abuse prevention? (Austin et al., 1982)   **Y N**

Goals and Objectives

21. What are the program's goals?
22. What are the program's objectives?

Are the program goals in writing, and do they specify the problem to be addressed, the target population to be reached, the desired outcome, and the service delivery approach? (Austin et al., 1982)   **Y N**

Are program goals reassessed annually?   **Y N**

Does a mechanism exist for input from the community, consumers, and other agencies regarding revision of program goals and objectives? (Community Chest and Council of the Cincinatti Area, 1980)   **Y N**

Are program objectives stated in concrete, measurable terms? (Austin et al., 1982)   **Y N**

23. What is the program's theoretical framework?
24. What aspects of the program might hinder goal achievement?

Management Information System

25. What was the maximum number of clients enrolled in the program during the past year?
26. What is the average daily program enrollment?
27. How many clients does the program expect to serve in one year?

Does the program plan to serve a minimum of 20-25 families per year in order to be cost-efficient? (National Center on Child Abuse and Neglect, 1979b)   **Y N**

28. a. Is paperwork completed in a timely manner?

    ____ Yes

    ____ No

b. If yes, within what time frame? _____

29. Does the program have provisions for confidentiality of program records?

     ____ Yes

     ____ No

30. What type of data collection system does the program use?

     ____ Manual

     ____ Computerized/automated

31. How frequently are data tabulated?

32. What types of data must be collected for monitoring requirements?

Are data collected and tabulated on a regular, systematic basis so that time needed to complete monitoring reports is minimal?	Y N
Are staff able to summarize client data routinely without having to go through client files? (Posavoc & Carey, 1980)	Y N
Are client files kept securely locked so that they are not accessible to unauthorized personnel?	Y N
Does the program have and use client consent forms in order to release confidential information?	Y N

Physical Structure

33. Is the program and/or agency listed in the phone book, in both the white and yellow pages?

     ____ Yes

     ____ No

34. Are program offices accessible to the physically handicapped?

     ____ Yes

     ____ No

35. Is there a waiting area or playroom for children that is equipped with toys and/or books for a variety of ages?

     ____ Yes

     ____ No

Are program offices and waiting areas:	
Adequately lit	Y N
Adequately heated/cooled	Y N
Cleaned regularly	Y N
With adequate seating/space in waiting room	Y N
Is there a sign with the program name and location?	
Within view of passing cars	Y N
On building directory	Y N
On office door	Y N

For "Best Practice" points, add a point for each Yes answer checked.

Does the program collect sufficient data so that the program administrator is able to answer all the questions on this questionnaire without collecting additional data?

Total number of "Best Practice" points for entire Inputs Assessment Instrument (out of a possible 101)

Y N

For more information on how to use the best practice standards in evaluating the data collected with this assessment instrument, turn to the section "Selecting Evaluative Criteria" in Chapter 2.

Appendix 2.3

ESTABLISHING PROGRAM GOALS AND OBJECTIVES

Writing Clear Program Goals and Objectives

Program goals are a statement of what the program is trying to accomplish. In order to evaluate whether the program, as currently structured, is achieving its goals (outcome evaluation), the evaluator needs to know what the goals are. All child abuse prevention programs have the same ultimate goal: to prevent or reduce the incidence of child maltreatment. It is not enough, however, to leave it at that. As a long-range goal, an abuse-free society is a desired future state. Yet, achievement of this goal may be so far in the future that, in the short run, all existing programs may be considered failures if this is their only stated goal. Fortunately, all programs have other, more specific goals that state what part of the larger problem they are attempting to address.

In addition to providing specific guidance for the program planning process, goals and objectives also define what data should be collected on an ongoing basis. For example, a child assault prevention program may have a goal of increasing public awareness, as measured by the following objectives: (1) Children will be able to identify appropriate and inappropriate touches, and (2) parents will discuss with their children how they can protect themselves. Precisely defining these objectives not only ensures the consistent application of the program design, but also helps to identify the kinds of data necessary to assess the program's effectiveness.

The general question to ask in setting goals is "What is the program trying to do?" Goals may reflect different levels of desired outcomes. Some programs have goals that specify the individual's desired state at the end of participation in the program. For example, the goal of an information and referral program is "to ensure parents have sufficient resources to care for their children." This goal refers to both the time during which the parent is receiving program services, as well as a time period following program contact. After receiving information and referral services, does the parent continue to have sufficient resources a month or a year later?

Some program goals are limited to the time period of the program. A perinatal program, for example, aims "to ensure that all new mothers and infants receive all appropriate medical services during the first 18 months of the child's life." While the program would certainly advocate that children receive the proper medical services throughout childhood, this goal is limited to the duration of the program.

To develop program goals, the following information is needed:

- What is the problem being addressed?
- Who are the clients?
- What services will the program provide?
- What is the desired outcome of the program?
- What is the theoretical rationale for the program?

The information gathered in response to these questions will enable the program planner to state program goals clearly, provided very specific answers are obtained. For example, "the problem being addressed" should be more narrowly defined than merely "child abuse" or "lack of perinatal services." The problem should reflect a specific type of maltreatment that research indicates may be preventable through intervention.

In addition to stating goals, it is also essential to delineate program objectives. Objectives describe program activities in terms of measurable outcomes. In other words, objectives are operationalized program goals, or behavioral indicators of the changes that the intervention is expected to bring about. Table 2.3 lists sample goals and objectives to accompany these goals.

Program objectives can reflect either the process or the outcome of a program. *Process* objectives pertain to the internal operation of the program. This usually means a change in the *effort* spent on an activity and the efficiency of that effort. Process objectives are sometimes only indirectly related to the program's major goal. For example, a parent education program sets a process objective to increase the amount of training received by staff. This indirectly affects the goal of increasing knowledge of good parenting practices. In contrast, *outcome* objectives refer to changes expected in members of the target population themselves. For the same parent education program, increasing knowledge about normal child development and stress reduction techniques is an outcome objective.

Table 2.3
Program Goals and Program Objectives

Program Goals

To increase bonding between parent and child.

To increase knowledge of child development among adolescents.

To change attitudes towards children and child rearing.

Program Outcome Objectives

Adolescents will demonstrate significantly higher levels of knowledge of child development at the end of a child development course than they did at the beginning of the course.

Volunteer hours will increase by 10% after 6 months of Community Education.

Parents will score significantly higher on a parenting skills inventory after completing the parent education class.

Program Process Objectives

Community outreach activities will increase by 50% by the end of the year.

The number of counseling hours provided by each therapist will increase by 10% by the end of the month.

There are several ways to go about systematically defining program goals and objectives. As an example, the following step-by-step approach is adapted from Mager's (1972) *Goal Analysis*.

1. *Write down the program service to be provided.* If there are several programs, choose one to start with. A child assault prevention program will be used as an example in succeeding steps.
2. *Write down the target population.* For whom does the program provide services? State the target population in terms of age, residence, sex, or other characteristics. In this example, the group decides that children, parents, and teachers at six city public schools are to be the target population.
3. *Write down program goals.* Group members do this by answering the question: What is the program trying to do? In the example, the group suggests the following goals:
   - Increase teacher knowledge of signs of abuse.
   - Increase child awareness of "good touch" and "bad touch."

4. *Write down what would be convincing evidence that the goal had been achieved* (*objectives*). What would program participants need to say or do in order to convince someone that the goal had been achieved? To do this, the group needs to focus on one goal at a time. The group chooses to start with "increasing teacher knowledge" and decides the following would convince them this occurred:

- Teachers report children with signs of abuse.
- Teachers say they know the signs of abuse.
- Teachers discuss presentations with one another.

5. *Sort out the list*. This involves going over the list generated in Step 4 to get rid of duplications, look for statements that are goals and not objectives, and check to be sure these are things the target population could *say* or *do* to convince the group the goal was met.

After much discussion the group decides on the following:

- "Teachers report children who have signs of abuse." This is a goal more than an objective. Also, if no child shows signs of abuse, this does not mean the teacher did not learn the signs of abuse. The group rejects this as an objective.
- "Teachers say they know abuse signs." This can be measured with a posttest. It is restated and kept on the list as an objective.
- "Teachers discuss presentations with one another." The group decides that this, again, is more a goal than an objective. Unless the discussions were monitored, there would not be any way to measure whether knowledge had increased. This statement was returned to the goal list to be reconsidered later.

Thus, the group is left with one objective:

- Teachers receive higher scores after presentations than before them on instruments assessing knowledge of signs of child abuse.

6. *Rewrite each measure*. The group should specify the quality, nature, or amount of the objective needed to be assured that the goal has indeed been reached. The group needs to consider how they would measure the objective, and the time frame to use in measuring it. Since participation in many child abuse prevention and treatment programs is time-limited, a natural time frame is usually provided for completion of program objectives.

The group rewrites the objective as follows:

- Teachers will score significantly higher on a test measuring knowledge of child abuse after program participation. They will score significantly higher both immediately after the end of the program, and again one month later, than they do before participating in the program.

These steps are repeated for each goal statement, each target population and each program service.

Appendix 2.4

CONDUCTING A COMMUNITY NEEDS
ASSESSMENT

There are many methods of conducting a needs assessment; these vary in terms of time, costs, human resources and utility of the results. The methods described here are the most practical ones for the typical community-based agency. There is no universally preferred method. The choice will depend on the time, staff, and money available to devote to the needs assessment process.

Methods of Assessing Community Need

Social Indicators Analysis

Certain groups need some services more than other groups do. For example, families in which both parents work have a greater need for child care than families in which one parent stays home. A social indicators analysis involves examining certain demographic, social, and economic characteristics of an area, and using those characteristics to determine need (Felner & Alber, 1983). The data are typically gathered from census records or community surveys.

This type of needs assessment serves two purposes. First, it will enable program planners to determine the basis of need for the service. An area with a very low birth rate, for example, may generate relatively weak demands for perinatal services for first-time mothers. Second, a social indicators analysis will help to assess the "fit" of the program to the community. For example, a perinatal program should locate its office in a residential rather than commercial area of the city, or in an area where couples or families tend to live.

The social indicators one chooses to examine will depend, in part, on the type of prevention program offered. School-based programs might examine the size and ethnicity of the school-age population in order to determine the type and extent of services needed; information and referral programs might be interested in the socioeconomic status of the area residents in order to determine what types of referrals to make.

Stressful Life Events

This technique is a more specific instance of a social indicators analysis. Stressful life events are believed to heighten an individual's risk for maladaptive behavior. Primary prevention services are targeted to *groups* with high frequencies of these events, while secondary prevention services are targeted to *individuals* who experience excessive amounts of these occurrences. For example, a school-based primary prevention program would select schools in which a large proportion of children experience parental divorce, and would conduct abuse prevention programs for all students. In contrast, a secondary prevention program would focus on providing services to the individual children experiencing parental divorce. Typical stressful life events for a child include death, divorce, school transfers, and the birth of a sibling (Felner & Alber, 1983).

Key Informant Surveys

This method involves soliciting input from various community leaders, citizen groups, service providers, consumers of services, and administrative and government officials. The selection of these "key informants" is based on the extent of their familiarity with the community in question, with an aim to achieve a balanced diversity of perspectives. It is advisable to keep the list of key informants between 15 and 20, if it appears that these interviews will provide an adequate amount of information (Hagedorn et al., 1976; National Institute of Mental Health [NIMH], 1985). Among the types of groups and agencies frequently represented in a key informant survey are:

- Child protective services
- Local schools
- Local hospitals and health clinics
- YMCAs and YWCAs
- Community agencies and organizations
- Law enforcement and criminal justice agencies
- Child care providers
- Social service agencies
- Mental health services
- Substance abuse treatment services
- Self-help and consumer groups
- Parent and other citizen groups

Key informant surveys are usually conducted through the use of structured interviews. These interviews focus on the following questions:

- What are the most pressing problems facing the community at the present time, and how would you prioritize them in order of importance?
- What resources are available that address these problems?
- What needs do you see that are not being met, or what problems are not being addressed?
- What groups in the community get the least amount of help?
- Who most often gets left out of service provision?

The key informant survey not only yields important information about community needs, but also operates as a type of "public relations" tactic in that the increased contact it generates between program staff and local groups helps to build community support for a program's services (Hagedorn et al., 1976).

Client Surveys

Surveying individual clients (as opposed to representatives of consumer *groups* often included in Key Informant surveys) provides a different viewpoint on what service gaps exist in the community. The ideal procedure in conducting a client survey is to survey all clients of a given service. This is, however, often impractical due to the large numbers involved. Thus, client surveys usually involve some sampling procedures. One approach is to send questionnaires to a random sample of clients who received services during a particular time period, say, for example, all clients receiving services during the first three months of the year. Another approach is to survey *all* clients who were receiving services on a given date. A third method is to survey all clients, either as they enter the program or as they terminate the program, for a specified time period.The method chosen will partially depend on the number of clients the program serves, and how quickly they flow through the program.

General Household Surveys

This type of survey requires the collection of data from individuals who are not necessarily receiving program services. Obviously this is a more difficult, time-consuming, and costly method than client surveys since a greater effort is needed to reach potential respondents. However, it provides more complete information. Client surveys reflect *their* views and unmet needs, while a general household survey provides a representation of the needs of the larger community. The types of questions asked are similar to questions asked of clients or key informants: What services do they use? What services do they see as being in short supply? Who is or is not being served?

Chapter 8

ANALYZING THE DATA

ollection of information from cases, observations, and/or clients
a mass of raw data, that is, data that are not systematically
ed into an interpretable, understandable form. In this chapter,
es for making sense of raw data are presented. In the first
Meaningful Data Summaries, basic concepts and methods for
the data are discussed. Then, in the second section, different
ssible findings are explored. Strategies for interpretation of
gs and action guidelines are applied to a variety of possible
nay hold in evaluation research.

MEANINGFUL DATA SUMMARIES

have been collected, the evaluator will be inundated
ts and pieces of information. In raw form, the data are
less. A single test score from a client yields few, if
bout the effectiveness of a given therapeutic pro-
knowledge that the agency's procedure for provid-
orresponds somewhat to one specific Best Practice
tle useful information. The most straightforward
ious pieces of raw data useful is to summarize

arizing the data begins with clarification of the
to be summarized. The data collected may be

classified as either *qualitative* or *quantitative*. Qualitative data are definitions, written documents, descriptions of events, behaviors, and so on. Quantitative data are numbers (e.g., test scores, number of yes answers to a given question on a survey, number of times a client was observed to engage in a specified behavior during a service session, number of staff hours allotted to a given service during the week).

Often, evaluation research will involve both forms of information. An input evaluation, for example, in which an audit is conducted to compare agency goals and objectives to Best Practice Standards in the field, may obtain both qualitative data in the form of descriptions of any discrepancies found and quantitative data in the form of numbers of correspondences or points of agreement between the standards and the agency policies. Surveys and observations also frequently contain both qualitative data (e.g., open-ended comments or questions) and quantitative data (e.g., ratings and other forced-choice responses, frequencies of responses, or behaviors).

Qualitative and quantitative data are analyzed differently. Therefore, when both types of information are present in the data, they must be sorted into different data sets so that separate analyses can be carried out. This is a fairly straightforward procedure. For example, if responses to both open-ended and forced-choice questions constitute data, the open-ended responses would be analyzed qualitatively, and forced-choice questions would be analyzed using quantitative techniques.

Quantitative Data Analysis

The techniques for creating quantitative data summaries range the very simple to the extremely complex. In this discussion, so the simple, straightforward methods, known as *descriptive sta* are explained, and some graphic representations of these simple tics are depicted. Then, basic concepts underlying the use of *inf statistics* are explained. Finally, applications of some of these complex techniques are briefly identified and described with examples.

Descriptive Statistics

Descriptive statistics are basic techniques for summarizing In many cases, the data summary will consist of a single num include:

Appendix 2.5

BEST PRACTICE STANDARDS FOR PROGRAM INPUTS

Best Practice Standards	Action Guidelines
The majority of program staff should have experience working with the type of client population served by the program, or with this type of program (Peat et al., 1978).	If the majority of staff are unfamiliar with program area and client type, there could be problems in the service delivery. A great deal of supervision will be required of inexperienced staff.
Case managers should have at least three years' experience in the treatment of child abuse and neglect (Cohn & DeGraaf, 1982).	Revise job descriptions and hiring practices.
Staff should be sensitive to cultural and ethnic differences between staff and clients and among clients (Peat et al., 1978).	Employ staff with ethnic make-up similar to clients'. Provide staff with inservice cultural sensitivity training.
Volunteers should be recruited from local churches, service clubs, and charitable organizations (National Center for Child Advocacy, 1976).	Consider these sources for volunteers. Those from the local community are more likely to stay involved and have more in common with the client population than those from a distant community.

Best Practice Standards

One staff member should be responsible for coordinating volunteers (National Center for Child Advocacy,
1976).

Action Guidelines

Implement policy.

Best Practice Standards

Paraprofessionals and volunteers
should be used for the following services:
- providing transportation, child
  care, and interpreting services
- teaching child care and home management (Parent Aides)
- providing information about the
  agency and community resources
- tutoring (National Center for
  Child Advocacy, 1976)

Action Guidelines

Implement policy. If the agency uses
professionals to provide these services, the per client cost or per unit
cost of providing services will be
quite high. If the agency is not currently using volunteers or paraprofessionals, consider changing this. If
the agency uses volunteers, examine
what the volunteer staff does compared to the paid staff.

Best Practice Standards

Parent aides are appropriate for the
following situations:
- parents who have referred themselves
- families who are socially and psy-
  chologically isolated
- parents with low self-esteem
- families under stress who thus
  have potential for abuse
- young parents who need assistance
  with parenting
- chronic neglect cases where the
  neglect results from a lack of
  knowledge about appropriate child
  care (National Center for Child Advocacy, 1979a)

Action Guidelines

If parent aides are used in situations
other than these, examine how effective they are (outcome evaluation).
If the aides are not effective, change
client eligibility criteria to fit these
guidelines, or change the program to
one more suited to the clientele.

Best Practice Standards

Programs should plan to serve a minimum of 20-25 families (*Planning*,
1976).

Action Guidelines

It is likely that programs serving
fewer clients are not cost-efficient.
If fewer clients are being served,
conduct a Cost Analysis (process
evaluation) to assess cost per unit of
service, and determine if program
size can be increased.

Best Practice Standards

Caseload size per worker should be 20-25 families (Austin et al., 1982; Cohn & DeGraaf, 1982; *Planning,* 1976).

Programs that serve families should consider maintaining charts on each family member who is being served in the program (*Planning,* 1976).

Data should be collected and tabulated on a regular, systematic basis, so that the time needed to complete monitoring reports is minimal. Program staff should be able to summarize the client data routinely without having to go through client files (Posavoc & Carey, 1980).

Services of medical, psychiatric, psychological, legal, and educational consultants should be available for use by agency staff (Child Welfare League of America, 1960; National Center for Child Advocacy, 1976).

In a crisis nursery or emergency respite care program, the staff-child ratio should be no more than one to four.

Programs that serve a large geographic area should consider establishing satellite offices (*Planning,* 1976).

Action Guidelines

Terminate stable clients. Hire more staff or redistribute caseloads.

This is preferable to keeping one family chart, as it allows the tracking of individual progress as well as family progress.

Implement such a system. Seek technical assistance to develop a more efficient system if the program does not have the necessary expertise in-house.

It is likely that at some point the agency will need to consult one or more of these professionals. It is wise to have made arrangements with various professionals before their services are needed.

Increase staffing or decrease program enrollment to adjust to requirements.

If the program falls into this category and does not have branch offices, possible locations include public agencies (CPS offices or schools) and nonprofit agencies (churches, hospitals). Program services can be offered on a limited basis at the satellite office, or the full range of services can be offered.

Best Practice Standards	Action Guidelines
Clients should be able to get to program sites easily, inexpensively, and safely. – inexpensive public transportation – public transportation stops near program site – minimal parking costs – well-lit parking areas and bus stops (Child Welfare League of America, 1959)	To maximize accessibility, consider: – subsidizing transportation expense – transporting clients – cab or bus vouchers – shuttle between bus stop or parking lot and program site – escorting clients to and from site and bus stop or parking lot
Program offices and waiting rooms should be clean, well-lit, and at a reasonable temperature (Weiner, 1982).	If not, evaluate where problems occur (e.g., infrequent janitorial services, improper lighting, poor ventilation such that drafts are created), and address these areas as soon as possible.
Program locations should be easy to find. A prominent sign should be visible from the street; hotlines and business phone numbers should be listed in white & yellow pages (Weiner, 1982).	Implement policy. If visible signs present a hazard to the safety of clients or staff (as in shelter programs), the street address should at least be obvious and business phones listed.
Programs serving children or families should provide a play area, with toys and books for a variety of ages (Weiner, 1982).	Implement policy. Obtain furnishings and toys from secondhand shops or through donations.
Program services should be available outside of the standard 9 to 5, Monday through Friday work week. Agencies should maintain hours of service that are responsive to community needs (National Association of Social Workers, 1975).	Offer some or all services at other times (evenings and weekends). Schedule client appointments off the site at home, work, or school.
Clients should be aware of where and how to obtain crisis intervention, referrals, or other services 24 hours a day (*The Role of the Mental Health Professional*, 1976).	Program staff can rotate on-call availability.

Best Practice Standards	Action Guidelines
A system should be established to handle emergencies. Programs not providing 24-hour coverage should arrange for another local agency to provide this service (*Planning & Implementing*, 1976).	Program staff should be aware of local 24-hour "hotlines" and provide these numbers to clients. Hotlines may include Crisis, Suicide Prevention, Respite Care & Child Protective Services.
Program staff should have a contact person at Child Protective Services to whom they can direct reports of abuse (Austin et al., 1982).	Meet with CPS staff. Discuss feasibility of setting up such a policy.
Program staff should have frequent contact with law enforcement, CPS, schools, hospitals, and other large public agencies (Austin et al., 1982).	Establish multidisciplinary team to meet monthly to discuss clients and programs. Invite representatives from these agencies to staff meetings to discuss their programs and their role in child abuse prevention.
Referral sources should be carefully identified and educated about the program's capacity and kinds of clients it plans to serve (*Planning*, 1976).	If it seems that a large percent of referrals are inappropriate, program staff should meet with referral source(s) to explain program eligibility requirements.
Clients should receive a comprehensive service package that addresses interpersonal and concrete needs of all family members. Clients should be assisted in locating needed community resources (Daro, 1985; National Center on Child Abuse and Neglect, 1979c).	Use inservice training to make staff aware of available services and to educate staff regarding potential range of client needs. Do case reviews to discover what types of service clients are not receiving; increase coordination with clients' case managers.

Best Practice Standards	Action Guidelines
The following data should be routinely collected and aggregated: – demographics of client population – services provided by agency and length of service provision – actual cost of services to date – staff characteristics and turnover (National Center for Child Advocacy, 1976)	Collect this data. If this information is not routinely collected or aggregated, preparation of reports is likely to be overly time-consuming.
Client records should be kept and should contain, at minimum, the following data (*Planning*, 1976; National Center for Child Advocacy, 1976): – client's age, sex, ethnic group, marital status, and family size – abuse history and high-risk indicators observed – treatment goals and time-limited objectives – reason for referral, referral source, and primary problem(s) – which staff are assigned to client and services being received – outcome of service at termination	Begin collecting this data.
Additional information beneficial to collect may include: – identity of primary caretaker – assessment of normal patterns of child care and any variations – description of family stress factors and reactions to these – evaluation of parent-child interaction	Begin collecting this data.

Best Practice Standards	Action Guidelines
Program goal statements should include the following: –desired outcome of program –client population to be served –problems addressed –service delivery approach (Austin et al., 1982)	Goal statements should be rewritten in this type of format. See "Writing Clear Program Goals and Objectives," Appendix 2.3.
Objectives should be stated in concrete, measurable terms (*Planning*, 1976).	Examine objectives and restate them in these terms.
Program goals should be reassessed annually (*Planning*, 1976).	If goals have not been reassessed in over a year, do this. It is important that program goals continue to reflect current client population, staff, and program services.

Appendix 2.6

DETERMINING UNIT COST

Defining Unit Cost

What does "unit of service" signify in concrete terms? The interpretation of this concept varies, depending on the information needs of the program. It usually refers to a single unit of time, or it could represent a single service endeavor (Hagedorn et al., 1976). For an agency that provides outpatient counseling services, for example, a unit of service may be defined either as a single counseling session, or as a counseling hour, which could involve two half-hour sessions.

The following table provides additional examples of possible service units for various types of programs.

Units of Service According to Type of Program

Type of Program	Unit of Service
Child care/respite care agency	One child care day
Residential treatment program	One community placement
Mental health agency	One hour of counseling
Parent Aide program	One home visit
Public awareness program	One program presentation
Parenting education program	One student; one class
Provider consultation service	One inservice training

Unit Cost as a Criterion Measure

Unit cost analysis can contribute in several ways to the evaluation of program inputs. Used by itself or in conjunction with data such as staffing ratios, the unit cost serves as a descriptive measure of program efficiency (Hagedorn et al., 1976). This is valuable information to have on hand, especially when agency administrators are in the process of making critical decisions concerning resource allocation or program development.

Unit cost analysis becomes even more meaningful, however, when used concurrently with other sets of criteria or with other types of evaluations (NIMH, 1985). When carried out along with a Process evaluation, the evaluator will be in a better position to determine why a unit of service costs what it does. Alternatively, unit cost information can be combined with an Outcome evaluation in order to determine the cost-effectiveness of an intervention.

The per unit cost of services can also contribute to the assessment of program inputs when used in concert with other evaluation criteria such as program goals and objectives, best practice standards, or community needs assessments. When combined with goals and objectives or best practice standards, the determination of unit cost can assist program planners to evaluate the feasibility of increasing or decreasing efforts to align program inputs more closely with these criteria.

When used together with a community needs assessment, unit cost analysis can serve to inform staff of the advisability of adjusting service provision efforts to meet levels of current need. For example, a high-cost service may be targeting a population group without much need for the service; conversely, a low-cost service may warrant expansion if the degree of community need far exceeds current levels of service.

In short, the determination of unit cost can greatly enhance the evaluation of program inputs. Some of the potential benefits of unit cost analysis include the following:

- Can serve to help justify continuing or increased allocation of resources to the program by the parent agency. Programs in which per-unit cost figures are readily available are more likely to receive additional funding than are those programs that have not clearly identified such costs.
- Allows for more efficient utilization of the agency facility by all of the agency's programs.
- Facilitates optimum allocation of staff among the agency's various programs.
- Enables the optimum scheduling of all program activities in operation within the agency.
- Assists in establishing optimum caseload or classroom sizes.
- Allows for a more direct comparison of the relative cost effectiveness of different programs.

The Determination of Unit Cost

The process of determining the cost-per-unit of service is essentially a four-step procedure. For the purposes of simplifying this discussion, it will be assumed that the program provides just one service; thus, "program" will be used interchangeably with "service." These four steps can be briefly summarized as follows:

1. The evaluator defines the unit of service for which cost is to be determined.
2. Data are collected to determine the total units of service provided by the program during a specified time period.
3. Data are collected to ascertain the total cost of the service for the same time period.
4. The total cost of the service is divided by the total number of service units to arrive at the per-unit cost.

It will be necessary to consult several sources of information in order to collect the data for Steps 2 and 3. Some of these sources may include:

- Account ledgers or journals
- Program and agency budgets
- Financial statements
- Grant and budget proposals
- Client logs
- Staff time sheets and time studies

This description of the computation process has been admittedly oversimplified in order to convey the general principles of unit cost determination. The completion of Step 3, in particular, can often be a complex and time-consuming process. The total cost of the program includes not only the direct costs of operation, such as staff salaries, materials, supplies, and maintenance of equipment and buildings used solely by the program, but also indirect costs, not directly attributable to a specific program, which are instead allocated to the program by the parent agency.

While the determination of per-unit costs can contribute valuable information to the evaluation effort, two caveats are in order. First, it is important to keep in mind that the per-unit cost of service is *not* necessarily equivalent to the cost of adding additional units of service. To determine the latter, one must also take into account the ratio between fixed program costs and variable program costs, as well as the likely stability of this ratio. Fixed costs, such as administrative costs, salaries, and building and maintenance expenses, are not likely to change much with incremental changes in numbers of service units provided. Variable costs, on the other hand, do fluctuate according to the level of service provided. These costs may be difficult to pinpoint, especially for newer programs, for programs in which the number of service units tends to be erratic and unstable, and in circumstances where future increases in costs are unpredictable.

Chapter 3

PROCESS EVALUATION

DEFINING THE EVALUATION QUESTION

A process evaluation focuses on program activities that involve direct interactions between clients and line staff and are central to the accomplishment of the program's objectives. This type of evaluation begins with an analysis of a program's service delivery system. The analysis requires identifying the program parameters and the major components therein. These components of the service delivery system form a series of distinct sequential events in which staff interact with other individuals in the system. In therapeutic programs, for example, the major components consist of referral, intake, client assessment, case planning, service provision, and termination. In school-based child assault prevention programs, the components would include service outreach/request, meeting with school administrator, teacher meeting, parent meeting, presentation to students, case advocacy, and follow-up. Beyond identifying the major program components, an evaluator needs to specify the activities, procedures, and routines that are performed within these components, as well as the timing of events, including the duration of the total program and the timing between discrete phases of the program. It is often helpful to identify program components and their relationships by drafting a flowchart of the service delivery system, a procedure described in detail in Appendix 3.1.

Process evaluations address the general issues: How well are we delivering our services? Are we doing what we intended to do? These issues frame more specific research questions, such as:

- How does our service delivery system impact on our clients?
- Are the services being delivered consistently to our clients as rendered by various staff?
- Is the timing between various phases of our service appropriate?
- Is client participation and input solicited in all phases of the service delivery system?
- What is the quality of the interaction between service providers and recipients?

Choosing Specific Variables

The process evaluation question needs to be operationally defined before a strategy for studying it can be devised. This entails translating abstract terms and concepts into concrete variables that are amenable to measurement. The following are several illustrations of how abstract process evaluation questions can be operationalized to yield relevant data. Table 3.1 examines a number of variables appropriate for a tertiary therapeutic program in which the evaluation question is "How does our service delivery system impact on our clients?"

The variables on this list are tailored to the type of service that is delivered. The list of variables is suggestive, but not exhaustive. On close examination of the sample case audit instrument in Appendix 3.2, one would doubtlessly be able to come up with additional variables that would reflect the service system's impact on clients.

To assess the impact of a program that serves multiple sets of clients, the evaluator must generate separate groups of variables corresponding to various service components. For instance, a school-based child assault prevention program typically interacts with the school principal, teachers, parents and children. For a comprehensive process evaluation of this program, one would have to examine service impact in relation to all of these parties. Table 3.2 provides an abbreviated list of variables that might be used in this case. These variables would have to be operationalized along the same lines as the example offered in Table 3.1.

Table 3.1

Examples of Specific Variables Appropriate for a Tertiary Therapeutic
Program

Variable:	Length of time from referral to service provision
Operationalized:	Number of days from referral to intake
Variable:	Continuity of staff
Operationalized:	Number of staff from whom clients receive services, start to finish
Variable:	Length of time in program
Operationalized:	Number of weeks in program, start to finish
Variable:	Level of client input
Operationalized:	Therapist's score on a 1-3 (high-low) scale of client's participation in case planning
Variable:	Frequency of client/therapist contact
Operationalized:	Number of person-to-person phone calls or face-to-face visits between client and therapist

LOCATING A PROCESS DATA COLLECTION INSTRUMENT

Published process instruments are relatively hard to come by compared to the abundance of outcome measures that appear in print. Nonetheless, there are a few instruments, primarily checklists, that can be found in books and manuals. Table 3.3 offers summaries of a few process measures that are available. A sample process instrument developed for use in a therapeutic treatment program, the Case Review Audit Instrument, is among those listed and appears in its entirety in Appendix 3.2.

SELECTING EVALUATIVE CRITERIA

Merely analyzing an intervention process does not constitute an evaluation of that process. In order to judge the merits of service delivery components, the results of this analysis must be assessed in light of relevant criteria such as best practice standards, agency policies, process goals, and client satisfaction.

Table 3.2

Examples of Specific Variables Appropriate for a Primary Prevention Program

---

School Principal

- Convenience of meetings with primary prevention staff
- Time spent relating to project staff
- Time spent intervening between project staff and school
- Length of program from onset to completion

Teachers

- Total amount of time spent on subject matter
- Perception of teacher trainings (e.g., length, time, punctuality, audience composition, etc.
- Perception of student presentations (see student category)
- Perceived burden on teachers

Parents

- Amount of information available regarding prevention program
- Notification regarding contact with children
- Perception of parent meetings (e.g., notice, convenience re time/location, punctuality, length, childcare, etc.)
- Accessibility of project staff to address questions/concerns

Children

- Punctuality of project staff's arrival
- Project staff's consideration of class rules and etiquette
- Ability of project staff to engage children
- Responsiveness to student questions and concerns
- Preparation of project staff

Best Practice Standards

Highly desirable operations and procedures in social work are often referred to as "best practices." These standards reflect current professional consensus about appropriate practice methods. Best practice standards suitable for assessment of an agency's service delivery may be found in the updated Child Welfare League of America Standards for Services for Abused and Neglected Children and Their Families and in other agency self-assessment manuals listed in Table 3.3. The FWRG Case Review Audit form, which appears in Appendix 3.2, incorporates best practice standards into the data collection instrument.

Table 3.3
Descriptions of Published Process Instruments

Title of Instrument:	Protective Services for Abused and Neglected Children and their Families
Source:	U.S. Government Printing Office, Washington, D.C. Prepared for Public Services Administration Contract No. SR S-500-76-005
Purpose:	Standards of best practice for structure and management of a comprehensive protective service program.
Description:	Two sets of checklists are featured — one for state protective service agencies and one for local protective service agencies. Areas covered include organization and staff structure; assessment, investigation, and validation; case management; services; resource development and interagency coordination; staff development; public education and information; and recordkeeping.
Title of Instrument:	Local Child Welfare Services Self-Assessment Manual, Part 1 Checklist
Source:	U.S. Department of Health, Education and Welfare National Center for Child Advocacy, Children's Bureau D.H.E.W. Publication No. 78-30518
Purpose:	Self-assessment tool for evaluating child welfare services in a local social service program.
Description:	Checklists in question format are presented covering the following areas: emergency/protective services; intake/service choice; in-home services; foster-family care; adoption services; residential group care; and case management/administration.
Title of Instrument:	Initial Interview Checklist
Source:	Gambrill, Eileen *Casework: A Competency-Based Approach* Englewood Cliffs, NJ: Prentice Hall (1983) pp. 429-431
Purpose:	An assessment of the quality of the client intake stage. Can be used as a model to develop a checklist of subsequent stages.
Description:	Six major categories encompassing many smaller tasks and services to be done during intake with clients.
Title of Instrument:	Checklist for Reviewing Nonverbal Behavior
Source:	Trower, Brant, and Argyle *Social Skills and Mental Health* Pittsburgh: University of Pittsburgh Press (1978)
Purpose:	An assessment of aspects of an individual's physical presence. Could be applied to evaluation of the style and manner of presenters in a primary prevention program.
Description:	Checklist covering nine qualities of physical behaviors (e.g., facial expression, posture, gestures). Space for indicating how variable should be altered.

(Continued)

Table 3.3

Descriptions of Published Process Instruments (Continued)

Title of Instrument:	Program Evaluation Form
Source:	Austin, Michael J.
	Evaluating Your Agency's Program
	Newbury Park, CA: Sage (1982)
	pp. 90-91
Purpose:	Client satisfaction survey elicits feedback on both process and impact of program.
Description:	Four questions. A combination of open-ended questions and Likert scales.

Agency Policies and Procedures

Sometimes a process evaluation is called for to determine the extent to which an agency has implemented services according to plans, that is, to what extent the agency has adhered to its own policies and procedures regarding service delivery. The FWRG Written Policies and Procedures Audit form, which appears in Appendix 3.3, was developed to elicit information on written agency policies and procedures. This information on policies and procedures serves as a yardstick against which to compare agency practices.

Process Goals

All agencies have program goals and objectives that specify the types of services and outcomes that they hope to accomplish. In addition, an agency may also prepare annual *process* goals and objectives that pertain to its internal operations. These objectives are appropriate criteria for a process evaluation. Examples of a few process objectives are:

- to reduce the amount of time people must spend on a waiting list for services by 25%;
- to increase the frequency of direct contact that therapists have with their clients by 15%;
- to terminate 10% of the total agency caseload this year.

Client Satisfaction

Client satisfaction can be measured in relation to program inputs, process, and outcomes. In a process evaluation, the focus of concern is on clients' assessments of the manner in which services were delivered to them. Published client satisfaction instruments often contain questions about inputs, process, and outcomes.

PROCESS EVALUATION CASE EXAMPLES

Interagency Coordination/Family Support Program

This program, housed within a county Developmental Disability Center (DDC), was developed in order to improve services to families of children with developmental disabilities who were also at risk, or victims, of abuse and neglect. The families had open cases both at DDC as well as at the county Department of Social Services (DSS). Despite receiving services from two sources, the general perception of workers was that these families were underserved by both systems. Workers were reluctant to establish responsibility for these cases because they were not familiar with both sides of the problem condition or the alternative services being received.

The program designed to address the needs of this client population had a twofold focus: the provision of intensive direct services to families and increased responsiveness and coordination between DDC and DSS. Program elements included (1) a direct service package consisting of a specialized case management home visitor treatment team, respite care for the DD child and siblings, and referrals to specialized services; (2) an interagency case screening and consultation team used to identify appropriate cases for service; (3) cross training of DDC and DSS staff; and (4) the implementation of a previously drafted interagency working agreement.

Agency Evaluation Proposal

The original evaluation proposal of this agency was to conduct an outcome evaluation of the case management component of their services. The proposed focus would have been an assessment of the impact of the intensive casework services provided to the families as measured by changes in characteristics known to be risk factors for child abuse and neglect. This initial interest changed as a result of a discussion with a major stakeholder, who was also the project's funding source and the party requesting the evaluation. In the funder's view, the project's most innovative aspect was the attempt to facilitate systems change through the implementation of an interagency coordination agreement. The change in focus from treatment to service coordination led to a change in the type of evaluation from outcomes to process, with a shift in the unit of analysis from client families to the service delivery system.

Evaluation Question

The process evaluation addressed the question: Does the cross training of workers and implementation of the interagency working agreement improve coordination between the DDC and DSS in providing services to families where there is risk of or actual abuse and neglect and one or more children are developmentally disabled?

Study Design

When the research question was operationalized, four major indicators of improved coordination emerged. These were an increase in line workers' level of knowledge, an increase in cross-agency referrals, an increase in the percentage of cross-agency referrals that result in open cases, and compliance with interagency protocols.

To enable measurement of the above variables, three strategies were developed. To measure change in line workers' knowledge regarding developmental disability, child abuse and neglect risk factors, and appropriate procedures for cross-agency referrals, a pretest and a posttest questionnaire were administered to all staff who participated in the project's training sessions. An analysis of cross-agency referral patterns was conducted by reviewing all pertinent cases in the data base of the DDC management information system prior to, during, and after the program. Compliance with interagency protocols was measured by auditing a randomly selected sample of client cases (n = 10) at three points in time: pre-, mid-, and post-implementation.

Data Collection Instrument

Two sets of instruments had to be created. The first set involved pretests and posttests to be administered to workers who received training. Two versions of the instrument were drafted, one for DDC workers emphasizing child abuse and neglect and DSS systems information and one for DSS workers emphasizing developmental disability and DDC systems information. Both versions contained items soliciting the workers' subjective impressions of intergroup relations between the two agencies. The second measurement tool developed was a case audit instrument organized according to direct service stages (e.g., referral, eligibility, program planning) within which appeared the interagency coordination protocols specific to each stage.

Data Collection

In an attempt to measure the full scope of interagency coordination, DDC originally sought to audit mutual client files of DDS in addition to their own. When these efforts were met with an insurmountable confidentiality barrier, the practical boundaries of DDC's self-evaluation became clear. What the agency could evaluate was its own compliance with the interagency coordination protocols, as well as its achievements in interagency training. The testing and data collection of pertinent MIS information was done by a DDC evaluator.

Data Analysis

Both quantitative and qualitative methods of data analysis were used. Pretest and posttest scores on the training measure were calculated using standard deviations and a t test. The open-ended test items, which asked for staff views and opinions, were analyzed qualitatively. The results showed a statistically significant difference between pretest and posttest scores. An analysis of the data base of MIS demonstrated a significant increase in the number of cross-referrals, as well as in the number of incoming referrals that resulted in open cases. Finally, a quantitative analysis of responses on the case audit forms yielded total scores on every audited case, an average of scores on all audited cases, and a breakdown of scores by service phases. These scores revealed an overall increase in compliance with the interagency protocols.

Utilization of Findings

A final report of the evaluation was submitted to the funding agents who requested the evaluation. A copy of the final report was given to the agency's counterpart in this project, the child protective service unit at DSS. An oral presentation of the findings was made at an in-service to both staffs. A summary of the project, the interagency protocols, and the findings were given wider dissemination through the Regional Center network. With respect to internal application of the findings, DDC incorporated the information they obtained into operational decision making and planning. Much of the information was used as a feedback loop to identify strong and weak areas of the interagency coordination effort.

Family Respite Program

Located in a rural area, this program offered respite services, a parent support group, a lending library, and in-home counseling and parent training for a period of up to two years to families at risk of abuse and neglect. The at-risk families were those in which members experienced excessive stress and/or lacked effective parenting skills. With two counseling staff, the program served approximately twenty families at any given time.

The in-home counseling and parent training component consisted of two-hour weekly or biweekly visits with the families with the children present in the home.Workers set goals with parents and discussed ways to meet them. The services delivered during these visits included training on the fundamentals of parenting and alternative disciplinary techniques, distributing written materials and role modeling proper parenting responses. The goal of the in-home counseling component was to assist parents in increasing their knowledge of child development, their parenting and coping skills, and their ability to use community resources effectively.

Agency Evaluation Proposal

The respite care program wanted to limit the scope of their evaluation to their in-home counseling services. In their initial proposal, they expressed an interest in conducting both a process evaluation, which examines the service delivery system and its effects on clients, and an outcome study, which assesses the short- and long-term impact of their services on their clientele.

Evaluation Question

At the outset, it was essential for this program, which had relatively few resources to devote to research, to identify a single evaluation focus, either process or outcomes. A careful inventory of the prerequisites for each type of evaluation revealed that a process evaluation was more feasible at that time than an outcome evaluation. The reason for this was that an audit of service delivery on a case-by-case basis can be conducted if there is a consistent system of case documentation. The agency had such case documentation, which allowed for a process evaluation to be conducted at a fairly low cost. An outcome evaluation would have been more complicated and costly. The in-home counseling program offered highly individualistic goals and treatment rather than a set curriculum and goals. Goals were often stated in vague terms rather than in measurable criteria. The program was not utilizing any standardized reporting measures of progress, such as goal attainment scales. Under these circumstances, the agency staff were not in a good position to conduct either a client-level or a group-level outcome study.

Study Design

In operationalizing the process evaluation, the study focused on the structure and organization of service delivery efforts, the consistency of service delivery to all clients regardless of the worker involved, the extent of case documentation, the type of direct services delivered, the frequency of contact, and the level of client input regarding the services delivered. This information was retrieved by doing an audit of case records. A decision was made to do a purposive sample of cases in order to review both a range of workers' files and select cases that covered the breadth of services from intake to termination. Best practice standards were the formal criteria against which the data were compared. Tacit agency protocols of practice were also compared to the data. These choices were made because the agency lacked written agency policies and procedures.

Data Collection

Using the FWRG Case Review audit instrument and the Written Policies and Procedures instrument (in Appendices 3.2 and 3.3), audits were conducted by two line workers, the agency director, and an evaluation consultant. These staff had to be trained in use of the data collection forms to ensure consistent responses. Working two full days, they collected data on fifteen cases.

Data Analysis

A qualitative analysis was used to examine the correspondence between audit data and tacit protocols of practice. Quantitative analysis involved tabulating responses according to service delivery phase, best practice standards, and worker. Cumulative calculations, including averages, on variables of interest were obtained, such as frequency of client-worker contact, level of client input, type of direct services, and degree of documentation. In measuring the correspondence of agency practices to best practice standards, the program demonstrated 32% compliance, 48% noncompliance, and 20% nondocumentation. The program excelled in the areas of staff contact and continuity, interagency case coordination, and client input. It was weakest in the area of client reassessment and client follow-up beyond termination.

Utilization of Findings

A written report described the findings of the evaluation, which were organized according to the phases of service delivery contained in the data collection instrument. The report focused on the extent to which services reflected best practice standards and tacit agency protocols, and it was shared with the board. The evaluation had a large impact on this program. Information about common practices and the best practice standards contained in the case audit form contributed toward the formulation of written agency policies and procedures. The review of the agency's readiness to conduct an outcome study helped to clarify the program's mission, goals, and methods, and led to adoption of goal attainment scaling (discussed in Chapter 4) as an aid to the delivery of services and assessments of client progress.

Appendix 3.1

FLOWCHARTING

A flowchart is a diagram of a logical sequence of activities or operations. Flowcharts are an efficient method of portraying complex phenomena in terms of simpler components.

There are legitimate differences in the various ways in which a process can be represented in flowcharts. No single flowchart represents the only way to depict a particular process; hence, no two analysts would necessarily produce identical diagrams. The purpose of this flowcharting exercise is to assist in conceptualizing a program's process.

In designing a flowchart, three issues in analysis and documentation must be resolved somewhat arbitrarily, but defensibly. These are:

- The temporal and action boundaries of each process must be identified, determined, and defined. With what events does this process begin and end?
- The "main line" or critical path of each program process must be determined and defined. The "main line" in your program is that series of activities and events that are the most critical within the process and involve direct interactions between clients and line staff.
- The amount and range of detail to be included in the documentation must be determined.

The following outline of tasks will guide the reader in how to draft a flowchart of an agency's process.

Task #1

Familiarize yourself with the International Standardized Flowchart Symbols in Exhibit A.

You should glance at these symbols, although you will probably only have occasion to use the process   , decision   , interrupt   , and possibly, documentation   symbols.

Task #2

Make a sequential list of the broad phases of your agency's service delivery.

Programs can be conceived of as having major phases in their respective service delivery systems, within which many smaller incremental procedures and activities are conducted. These broad phases may be, for instance, referral, intake, case assessment, case planning, service provision, and termination. Or an alternative might be referral, pre-service, service, and follow-up. These phases naturally will vary from program to program, depending on the nature and structure of the services offered. The titles of the broad phases are not standardized and are up to the discretion of the individual drafting the flowchart. List these phases logically and sequentially on a piece of paper.

Task #3

Make a sequential list of the principal activities in your agency's service delivery system.

Using the aforementioned list of phases of your service delivery system as a guide, generate from it another list of the principal activities, direct and indirect, that comprise your agency's process. List them in logical, sequential order.

Task #4

Reviewing the list of principal activities, indicate next to each which are direct (D) and which are indirect (I).

The direct activities are those that involve interaction between the staff and clients. These will eventually appear as rectangles on the "main line" of the flowchart. The indirect activities do not involve direct interaction between staff and clients, but are procedures that sustain the direct activities and are integral to the program's process. These will be represented by various symbols other than the rectangle and will appear one step off the "main line."

Exhibit A

IBM Flowcharting Template – International Standardized Flowchart Symbols

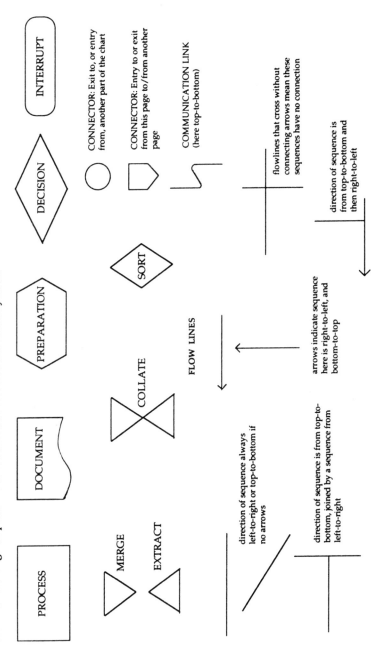

PROCESS

DOCUMENT

PREPARATION

DECISION

INTERRUPT

MERGE

EXTRACT

COLLATE

SORT

CONNECTOR: Exit to, or entry from, another part of the chart

CONNECTOR: Entry to or exit from this page to/from another page

COMMUNICATION LINK (here top-to-bottom)

FLOW LINES

flowlines that cross without connecting arrows mean these sequences have no connection

direction of sequence is from top-to-bottom and then right-to-left

arrows indicate sequence here is right-to-left, and bottom-to-top

direction of sequence always left-to-right or top-to-bottom if no arrows

direction of sequence is from top-to-bottom, joined by a sequence from left-to-right

Task #5

Chart your agency's service delivery process following the guidelines presented below.

Transcribe the steps you have previously listed in diagram form. The following procedures describe how to diagram the flowchart. Refer to Exhibit B and Exhibit C when reading each of the following points.

1. Draw a horizontal double line to represent the "main line" or critical path. The direction of the sequence is always shown left to right and top to bottom unless lines with arrows point in other directions.
2. Indicate the beginning of the program process and your flowchart by printing START at the beginning of the double line.
3. Place a vertical line immediately after START. Insert vertical lines at the beginning and end of all phases or segments of the program process.
4. Referring to your sequential list of activities, place each one of these distinct activities that involve direct interaction between your staff and clients (e.g., initial school contact, introductory principal meeting) in a rectangle on the double line.
5. Place those activities *not* involving direct activities, but rather indirect activities, one step off the "main line." These indirect activities are the procedures for coordinating, guiding, monitoring, or supporting participants and activities and are integral to the process being diagrammed (e.g., reporting procedures, filing procedures, supervisory and review processes, support services). Use appropriate symbols as represented in Exhibit A. Any symbols may be used to denote various types of steps or activities, however, the fewer the better. Each symbol should have a uniform meaning in a single chart or set of charts. Symbols that conform to established meanings of the International Standardized Symbols do not need to be keyed.
6. Be concise, but representative, in listing the distinct activities of your agency's service delivery process on the diagram; the beauty of flowcharting lies in its simplicity.
7. Number sequentially each one of the steps, on and off the "main line." This is for the sake of clarifying the temporal order of the activities.
8. Indicate the completion of the program process and your flowchart by printing END at the end point on the double line.
9. Directly beneath the "main line" draw a single horizontal line equal to the length of the "main-line." Bring the vertical lines, indicating phases of the process, down to the lower horizontal line. Give these phases Roman numerals and the titles that you used in Task 2 above. Next to the titles, indicate how long those phases last in theory.
10. Under the horizontal line depicting the appropriate phase, list the numbers of the process steps contained therein, with the job titles of staff charged with implementing those activities.
11. Scan your chart for blatant errors and then congratulate yourself for you are finished.

Sample Schema of the "Main-Line" of a   Exhibit B
Direct-Service Program Process

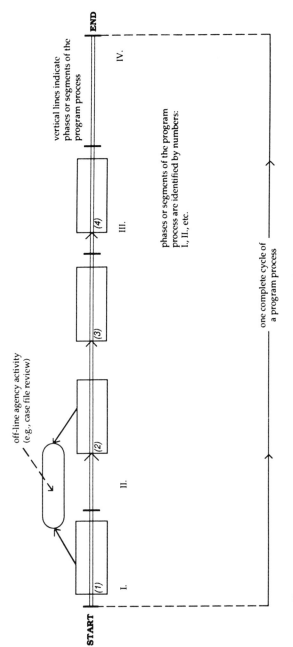

off-line agency activity
(e.g., case file review)

vertical lines indicate
phases or segments of the
program process

phases or segments of the program
process are identified by numbers:
I, II, etc.

one complete cycle of
a program process

Key: rectangles represent major activities or subroutines involving direct interaction of clientele and line staff through program
       process--each is numbered for reference and specification
       connecting lines represent lines of communication or other relationship, with arrows indicating directions

Exhibit C

Everytown Senior Center
Community Senior Services (CSS) Program
Program Process Flowchart

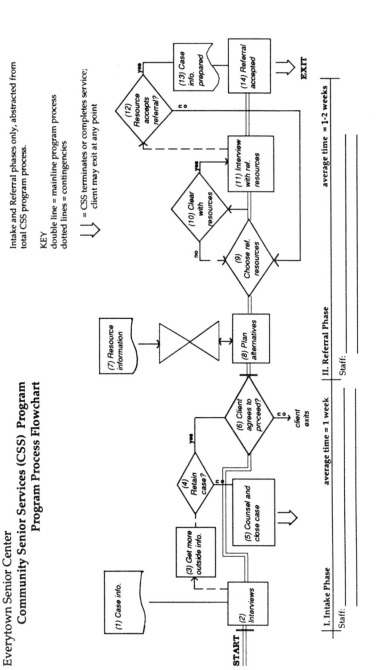

Intake and Referral phases only, abstracted from total CSS program process.

KEY
double line = mainline program process
dotted lines = contingencies

⇒ = CSS terminates or completes service; client may exit at any point

RECAP OF FLOWCHARTING PROCEDURES

1. Familiarize yourself with the International Standardized Flowchart Symbols.
2. Make a sequential list of the broad phases of your agency's service delivery.
3. Make a sequential list of the principal activities in your agency's service delivery.
4. Reviewing the list of principal activities, indicate next to each which are direct (D) or indirect (I).
5. Chart your agency's service delivery process.

CASE REVIEW AUDIT

Case #: _____

Review Date: _____

Reviewer: _____

DIRECTIONS: First, photocopy a sufficient number of copies of this blank audit form to use with your sample. In completing the form, use simple, concise phrases. In the column next to the items appearing in the audit form below, place a + if the practices in a case correspond to your agency's written policies and procedures or *best practice standards* and a – if the practices do not reflect your policies or *best practice standards*.

+/–	I. REFERRAL
	Staff Who Provided This Service:_____ _____ _____
	Who made the referral (e.g., client, court, hospital, etc.)? Did someone need to follow up the referral? If so, who was it? How soon, after the initial phone call, was the referral followed up? What happened administratively with the referral after the follow-up contact?

+/−	I. REFERRAL (cont.)
	Where does documentation of this phase appear in this client's record?
	Was the client contacted on the same day that the referral was received? (Cohn & DeGraff, 1982) Y N N/A Was the referral source consulted for background information on the case? (Cohn & DeGraff, 1982) Y N N/A
	II. INTAKE
	Staff Who Provided This Service:_____ _____ Who decided that this client was eligible for services? Which of the agency's eligibility criteria did this client demonstrate? How was this client's eligibility established? How long after the referral was the eligibility determination made? Where does documentation of this phase appear in this client's record?
	Was there a significant amount of contact with this client prior to the completion of intake? (BPA, 1977) Y N N/A Was there a significant amount of contact with household members prior to the completion of intake (BPA, 1977) Y N N/A Was there a significant amount of contact with other agencies prior to the completion of intake? (BPA, 1977) Y N N/A Was it made clear to this client what the program was going to do for/to them? (BPA, 1977) Y N N/A Was informed consent obtained from this client to obtain material from other agencies and individuals? (Peat et al., 1978) Y N N/A

+/−	III. WAITING LIST
	Staff Who Provided This Service:_____ _____ Was this client placed on a waiting list initially for services? Who put the client on the waiting list? How long did this client remain on the waiting list?
	IV. CLIENT ASSESSMENT
	Staff Who Provided This Service:_____ _____ _____ _____ _____ Was a formal assessment ever done on this client? When and how often was this client assessed? How long (i.e., number of days, weeks) did this (these) period(s) of assessment last? Who did the client assessment? What aspect of this client was assessed (e.g., behavior, knowledge, attitudes, skills, interpersonal functioning, needs, etc.)? What methods were used to assess this client? Did the client or client representative give input? Where does documentation of this phase appear in the client record?
	Was the client involved in an examination of factors that could contribute to abuse and neglect? (Daro, 1985) Y N N/A Was a conjoint family interview done to evaluate a family inter-action? (BPA, 1977) Y N N/A Do feedback loops exist to revise the diagnostic assessment? (Peat et al., 1978) Y N N/A

+/−	V. SERVICE CASE PLANNING
	Staff Who Provided This Service:_____ _____ _____ _____
	Was case planning done for this client? How frequently was case planning done for this client? What information was considered in planning for this client (e.g., client assessments, progress, strengths and weaknesses, altered circumstances, etc.)? What was the planning process like (e.g., client present, multidisciplinary team, formal planning meeting, etc.)? In planning for the client, were services coordinated with other service providers? If so, how? How was the service plan written (e.g., behavioral/psychodynamic, measurable/ nonmeasurable, etc.)? Did the client or client representative give input? To what degree? How? Where does documentation of this service appear in the case record?
	Was a multidisciplinary team used? (BPA, 1977) Y N N/A Were the treatment goals realistic, measurable, nonambiguous outcome statements? (BPA, 1977) Y N N/A Was the service plan based on diagnostic assessment? (Peat et al., 1978) Y N N/A Was the service based on utilization of agency and community resources? (Peat et al., 1978) Y N N/A Did the treatment plans specify services to be offered? (BPA, 1977) Y N N/A Did the treatment plans specify who will provide them? (BPA, 1977) Y N N/A Were the service goals geared to the client's ability to achieve them? (Peat et al., 1978) Y N N/A

+/−	V. SERVICE CASE PLANNING (cont.)

Were expectations of the client, reflected in the case plan, made clear to the client? (Peat et al., 1978) Y N N/A

Was the initial case service plan completed within 90 days of the initial application or referral? (Peat et al., 1978) Y N N/A

Do feedback loops exist to modify the case service plan? (Peat et al., 1978) Y N N/A

VI. SERVICE PROVISION

Staff Who Provided This Service:_____

_____

_____

_____

_____

Who initiated contact most of the time, client or worker?

How frequent was contact typically made?

What services were provided to this client?

Where does documentation of the services provided appear in the client's record?

Was client contact made at least weekly? (Cohn & DeGraff, 1982) Y N N/A

If this client was referred to other agencies for services, were referrals followed up to ensure that contact was made? (BPA, 1977) Y N N/A

Was contact with other providers maintained at least monthly? (Community Research Applications, Inc.) Y N N/A

Was contact with other providers made weekly in times of crisis or unusual circumstances? (Community Research Applications, Inc., 1977) Y N N/A

+/−	VII. TERMINATION
	Staff Who Provided This Service:_____
	Has this case been terminated?
	Who initiated the termination, client or staff?
	What was the basis for the termination?
	How was this termination handled procedurally?
	Was this client referred to other agencies? through the client or directly?
	Did the client or client representative give input to the worker about his/her termination?
	What happened to the case record at the agency?
	Where does documentation of this phase appear in the client's record?

	Was this client's case terminated at the peak of his/her progress? (BPA, 1977)	Y N N/A
	Were all other service providers notified of the termination? (Urban Institute, 1979)	Y N N/A
	Was the client prepared for termination well in advance of its occurrence? (BPA, 1977)	Y N N/A

VIII. CLIENT FOLLOW-UP
Staff Who Provided This Service:_____   _____   _____   _____
Who was the staff person who followed up with the former client?
How long after the case was initially closed did the first follow-up contact with this client occur?

+/−	VIII. CLIENT FOLLOW-UP (cont.)
	How long did follow-up continue? Has the former client stabilized, progressed, or regressed since his/her case was closed? Has this client's case been reopened as a result of follow-up contacts? Where does documentation of this service exist? in the client's case record?
	Has there been follow-up with this client since the case was closed? (BPA, 1977) Y N N/A Was the client's progress monitored during follow-up? (BPA, 1977)) Y N N/A

_____ NO. OF +'s

_____ NO. OF −'s

_____ NO. OF STAFF INVOLVED WITH CLIENT FROM START TO FINISH

_____ DEGREE OF CLIENT INVOLVEMENT IN THE PLANNING PROCESS
1 (VERY INVOLVED) TO 5 (NOT VERY INVOLVED)

_____ TOTAL NO. OF AFFIRMATIVE RESPONSES TO BEST PRACTICE STANDARDS
(29 POSSIBLE)

Appendix 3.3

WRITTEN POLICIES AND
PROCEDURES AUDIT

DIRECTIONS: Complete the following audit form with short, concise phrases reflecting policies in place at your agency. If you have written policies and procedures, refer to them. The questions in bold print represent best practice standards in the field of social welfare. Indicate whether those standards are reflected in your policies and procedures by circling yes (Y), no (N), or non-applicable (N/A).

I. REFERRAL
Policy/procedures in writing?   Y N
Who in the community (i.e., clients, professionals) are appropriate referral sources?
Who is the designated person at the agency to accept the referral?
Who at the agency is designated to follow up the referral?
How soon (i.e., number of hours/days) is the referral to be followed up?
What are possible courses of action to take with a referral after the follow-up contact has been made?
What documentation of this phase should appear in the client's record?

I. REFERRAL (cont.)

Will the client be contacted on the same day that the report is received? (Cohn & DeGraff, 1982)	Y N N/A
Will the referral source be consulted for background information on the case? (Cohn & DeGraff, 1982)	Y N N/A

II. INTAKE

Policy/procedures in writing?   Y   N

Who at the agency is designated to decide if a referred party is eligible for services?

What are the agency's eligibility criteria?

How should eligibility be established (i.e., written documentation, observation, client information, etc.)?

Are there designated timelines within which to make an eligibility determination? If so, what are they?

What documentation of this phase should appear in the client's record?

Is a significant amount of contact with the client required prior to the completion of intake? (BPA, 1977)	Y N N/A
Is a significant amount of contact with household members required prior to completion of intake? (BPA, 1977)	Y N N/A
Is a significant amount of contact with other agencies required prior to completion of intake? (BPA, 1977)	Y N N/A
Will it be made clear to the clients what the program is going to do for/to them? (BPA, 1977)	Y N N/A
Will informed consent be obtained from clients to obtain material from other agencies and individuals? (Peat et al., 1978)	Y N N/A

III. WAITING LIST

Policy/procedures in writing?   **Y   N**

Who at the agency is designated to place someone on the waiting list?

Who at the agency is the designated person to manage the waiting list?

Is there a limit as to how long someone can remain on the waiting list?

IV. CLIENT ASSESSMENT

Policy/procedures in writing?   **Y   N**

Is it the agency's intention to conduct formal client assessments on every client?

Who is the designated staff person to assess a client?

What aspects of the client are being assessed (i.e., client needs, knowledge, skills, behavior, attitudes, interpersonal functioning, etc.)?

What are the recognized methods of client assessment (e.g., testing, observation, client self-report, family report, etc.)?

When and how often should the client be assessed? Is client reassessment regularly conducted?

How long should this period of assessment last for a client?

What opportunities theoretically exist for client input? What recourse does the client have if she/he disagrees with the assessment?

What documentation of this phase should appear in the client record?

Should the client be involved in an examination of all
factors that may contribute to abuse or neglect?
(Daro, 1985)   **Y   N   N/A**

Should evaluations, including a conjoint family interview, be
done to evaluate family interaction (BPA, 1977)   **Y   N   N/A**

Do feedback loops exist to revise the diagnostic assessment?
(Peat et al., 1978)   **Y   N   N/A**

V. SERVICE CASE PLANNING

Policy/procedures in writing?   Y   N

Is it the agency's intention to do formal case plans?

Who at the agency is designated to do service planning for/with the client?

What information is considered in planning for the client (e.g., client assessments, needs, altered circumstances, progress, strengths, weaknesses, etc.)?

What is the planning process intended to be like (i.e., multidisciplinary teams, client present, etc.)?

How often is a service plan supposed to be done?

What is the designated format for the service plan?

Are services to be coordinated with other service providers? If so, is it specified how?

What opportunities theoretically exist for client input? Are clients consulted in drafting the case plan? Must they approve of the plan? What recourse do they have if they disagree with their service plan?

What documentation of case planning should appear in the client's record?

Will multidisciplinary teams do case review? (BPS, 1977)   Y   N   N/A

Do feedback loops exist to modify the case service plan?
(Peat et al., 1978)   Y   N   N/A

Is the initial case service plan completed within 90 days of the
initial application or referral? (Peat et al., 1978)   Y   N   N/A

Are treatment goals realistic, measurable, nonambiguous outcome
statements? (BPS, 1977)   Y   N   N/A

Are service plans based upon diagnostic assessment? (Peat et al.,
1978)   Y   N   N/A

Are service plans based on utilization of agency and community
resources? (Peat et al., 1978)   Y   N   N/A

Do treatment plans specify the services to be offered?
(BPA, 1977)   Y   N   N/A

V. SERVICE CASE PLANNING (cont.)

Do treatment plans specify who will provide the services?
(BPA, 1977)   Y N N/A

Are the service goals geared to the client's ability to achieve
them? (Peat et al., 1978)   Y N N/A

Are expectations of the client, derived from the service plan,
made clear to that client? (Peat et al., 1978)   Y N N/A

VI. SERVICE PROVISION

Policy/procedures in writing?   Y N

How frequent does client/worker contact need to be?

Whose responsibility is it to ensure that client/worker contact is maintained?

What services are to be provided?

How long can the client receive services?

What recourse does the client technically have if she/he is dissatisfied with the services?

What documentation of this phase is supposed to appear in the client record?

Is contact between case coordinator and client to be made at
least weekly? (Cohn & DeGraff, 1982)   Y N N/A

When clients are referred to other agencies for services, are
referrals to be followed up to ensure that contact was made?
(BPA, 1977)   Y N N/A

Is contact with other providers to be maintained at least
monthly? (Community Research Applications, Inc. [CRA],
1977)   Y N N/A

Is contact with other providers to be maintained at least
weekly in times of crisis or unusual circumstances?
[CRA], 1977)   Y N N/A

VII. TERMINATION

Policy/procedures in writing?   Y   N

On what basis would a client's case be terminated?

Whose decision is it to terminate a client's case? Does it require a supervisor's approval?

What are the appropriate procedures for terminating a client's case?

Are there provisions for making referrals of the client to other agencies on termination of the case?

What input do clients have in a decision about termination? What recourse would a client have if she/he disagrees with a particular decision?

What is to be done with client's records on termination from the agency?

What documentation of this phase should appear in the client's record?

Is the time between maximum progress and termination
minimized? (BPA, 1977)   Y   N   N/A

Are all other service providers to be notified of the
termination? (Urban Institute, 1979)   Y   N   N/A

Is the client to receive preparation by the agency for
termination well in advance of its occurrence?
(BPA, 1977)   Y   N   N/A

VIII. CLIENT FOLLOW-UP

Policy/procedures in writing?   Y   N

Is this service formally and routinely provided by the agency?

Who at the agency is designated to follow up former clients?

VIII. CLIENT FOLLOW-UP (cont.)

When is the follow-up to be initiated? How often is it scheduled to occur? For how long will it continue?

What action is to be taken by the agency if, in the course of a follow-up contact, it is learned that a former client has regressed?

Where would documentation of this service appear? If it is recorded in the client record, on what form does it appear?

Is follow-up contact to be initiated with clients after termination? (BPA, 1977)   Y   N   N/A

Is the client's progress to be monitored during follow-up? (BPA, 1977)   Y   N   N/A

_____   TOTAL NO. OF WRITTEN POLICIES AND PROCEDURES
         (8 POSSIBLE)

_____   TOTAL NO. OF AFFIRMATIVE RESPONSES TO BEST PRACTICE
         STANDARDS (29 POSSIBLE)

Chapter 4

OUTCOME EVALUATION: GROUP LEVEL

DEFINING THE EVALUATION QUESTION

Group level outcome evaluations assess the effects of a program's overall performance. These studies involve (1) collecting data on the same question(s) from different individuals, (2) aggregating the data, and (3) assessing the aggregated data to determine how the group, as a whole, responded.

The group level approach is usually employed if a program has well-defined goals for all clients that can be measured in the same way. An educational prevention program, for example, might be evaluated with respect to the effectiveness of its teaching the concepts of "good touch" and "bad touch." All children in the program would be asked the same questions, and a group profile of their understanding would be developed. Similarly, a respite care program whose goals involve improving family home conditions might be evaluated with regard to reducing the primary caretaker's social isolation. All primary caretakers in the study would be asked the same questions about their social contacts before and after participation in the respite program. This allows the evaluator to develop a group profile summarizing program-related changes in social behavior. The types of questions often addressed by group level outcome evaluations are:

- How successful is the program in teaching clients about a specific topic (e.g., age-appropriate behaviors)?
- How do the behavioral changes clients exhibit before and after a program compare with changes over time exhibited by people who do not experience the program?
- What do clients normally learn from the program?
- Does a program have the desired impact on most of the clients?
- Does the program have a long-term impact on the clients' behavior?

There are different types of group-level outcomes related to whether the preventive service is nontherapeutic, therapeutic, or educational in nature. Typical nontherapeutic programs address parenting practices, the living conditions of a family, or the economic status of a family. Changes in these and other similar problems between the time a client enters and leaves a program are the primary outcomes of interest. These desired changes are usually identified in a program's goals and objectives. Group-level outcomes frequently examined for nontherapeutic prevention programs are:

- expanding the number of child care options open to parents;
- improving the family's economic status;
- improving the conditions and safety of the family's housing;
- reducing the primary caretaker's social isolation;
- improving the family's ability to use other agency resources.

Therapeutic programs tend to address parent/child communication, family functioning, or the mental health of individual parents. Group-level outcomes frequently related to therapeutic prevention programs include:

- expanding the range of discipline strategies parents use with their children;
- improving the family's problem solving skills;
- improving the self-esteem of family members;
- reducing the primary caretaker's stress level;
- improving the parents' coping skills;
- improving the child's behavior;
- improving the family's ability to communicate;

- expanding the family's ability to cope in a crisis;
- facilitating the family's interactions with extended family and friends.

Educational child abuse prevention programs involve presentations to school groups, parents' groups, community groups, and others. These programs are intended to raise the level of awareness and social skills related to child abuse prevention. The degree to which a program attains its goals with selected populations is the primary outcome of interest. Goals frequently set by educational programs include:

- improving the child's ability to say "no" in potentially abusive situations;
- involvement of parents in school-based prevention programs;
- increasing a group's knowledge about child abuse;
- facilitating a child's ability to report abuse;
- improving a child's awareness that an abusive incident was not his/her fault.

Choosing Specific Variables

The variables selected for an outcome evaluation should be credible: They should be directly related to the goals and objectives of the program under evaluation and they should be clearly defined in terms of the measurements that will be gathered. For example, a general goal for an educational child abuse prevention program is "Does this program improve a child's ability to identify an abusive situation?" A more specific goal would be "Do children leave this program knowing how to distinguish between appropriate and inappropriate touches?" A number of concrete measures can be derived from this goal (e.g., Can children describe an appropriate touch? Can children define an inappropriate touch? How do children describe an "uh-oh" touch?).

A therapeutic program evaluation question might address the general goal of improving parenting skills. A more specific goal narrows the question by identifying one type of parenting skill, asking, for example, "Is the range of discipline strategies that a parent uses improved as a result of this program?" Operational variables for this question include (1) the number of times parents use a time-out strategy, (2) the number of times parents reason with the child, and (3) the number of different strategies a parent reports using during a specified time period. For additional examples of how evaluation questions may be operationally defined, see Table 4.1.

Table 4.1

Examples of Specific Variables Derived from Abstract and Specific Goals

I. *Abstract Goal:* Teach children how to protect themselves.
   A. *Specific Goal*: Teach children self-defense techniques.
      1. *Specific Variable:* Number of times children are observed using a specific self-defense technique during a specified observation session.
      2. *Specific Variable:* Number of children who can demonstrate a specific technique (presented in the program) to use when a stranger approaches.
   B. *Specific Goal:* Teach safety concepts.
      1. *Specific Variable:* Number of children who choose not to go with a stranger in a test situation.
      2. *Specific Variable:* Children's definitions of the concept "safety."

II. *Abstract Goal:* Improve Parenting Skills.
   A. *Specific Goal:* Teach parents about age-appropriate behaviors.
      1. *Specific Variable:* Number of age-appropriate behaviors a parent can identify.
      2. *Specific Variable:* Number of times a parent uses appropriate (or inappropriate) behavioral expectations to explain a child's behavior during a structured interview.
   B. *Specific Goal:* Improve understanding of children's and parents' roles in the family.
      1. *Specific Variable:* How parents score on an instrument such as a parenting index.
      2. *Specific Variable:* Parents' descriptions of roles for each family member.
   C. *Specific Goal:* Teach parents to use community resources to alleviate pressures.
      1. *Specific Variable:* Number of resources a parent can identify.
      2. *Specific Variable:* Number of different resources a parent uses in a one-month period.
      3. *Specific Variable:* Frequency with which a parent uses available resources in a one-week period.

III. *Abstract Goal:* Improve child's behavior.
   A. *Specific Goal:* Increase behavioral options in stressful situations.
      1. *Specific Variable:* Number of options a child can identify.
      2. *Specific Variable:* Number of options a child can model in a test situation.
      3. *Specific Variable:* A child's description of an appropriate response to a verbal reprimand (in a test situation).
   B. *Specific Goal:* Improve ability to socialize.
      1. *Specific Variable:* Number of times a child approaches other children in a nonthreatening manner during a specified observation session.
      2. *Specific Variable:* Number of different children a child approaches in a friendly manner during a specified observation session.
      3. *Specific Variable:* Children's definitions of the concept of friendship.
      4. *Specific Variable:* Children's demonstrations of the concept friendly in a test situation.

LOCATING AN OUTCOME DATA COLLECTION INSTRUMENT

There are a number of data collection instruments designed to measure group-level outcomes. A sample of these instruments is presented in Table 4.2. The categories that appear in Table 4.2 reflect the kinds of information that an evaluator should obtain when investigating the possible use of existing instruments. These include quality assessment data on reliability (i.e., the ability of the test to yield consistent scores), validity (i.e., the content of the test is truly representative of the variable(s) the test is supposed to measure), cultural sensitivity (i.e., the test is appropriate for use with different ethnic groups), and normative data (i.e., expected scores based on the sample used to develop the test).

The test-retest reliability of the instruments is represented as a number between 0.00 and 1.00, where 0.00 means that there is no relationship between scores for an individual who takes the test on two different occasions (i.e., the test is not reliable) and 1.00 means that scores for an individual who takes the test on two different occasions are identical (i.e., the test is 100% reliable). It is not expected that tests will have 100% reliability. It is, however, expected that tests will have some degree of reliability. Although the minimum standard may vary, a good rule of thumb is to be suspicious of reliability scores that fall below about 70%.

SELECTING EVALUATIVE CRITERIA

Appropriate selection of criteria for quantitative results in outcome evaluation research is crucial to the credibility of the study. Often the comparison standard for quantitative data is a statistical test to compare the results for two (or more) sets of scores (e.g., pretest-posttest or treatment and control groups; see Chapter 8, Inferential Statistics). The level of statistical significance and the appropriate statistical test should be established prior to beginning data collection. If the comparison standard for quantitative data is a set of minimum acceptable scores, then these scores and the rationale for their use should be specified.

In many cases, it is desirable to use measures of both statistical significance and substantive significance as reflected in minimum standards to interpret the findings. If only statistical tests are used, when a group's scores are found to be different the question remains whether

Table 4.2
Descriptions of Standardized Outcome Instruments

Title of Instrument:	Self-Esteem Inventories (Stanley Coopersmith, 1982)
Source:	Consulting Psychologists Press
	577 College Avenue
	Palo Alto, California 94306
	(415) 857-1444
Purpose:	Assess self-esteem of children, adolescents, and adults (8 years to adult).
Length of Test:	About 15 minutes.
Reliability:	Test-retest = .70.
Validity:	Documented extensively. See instruction booklet for details.
Cultural Sensitivity:	Different ethnic groups have been studied, including White, Black, Hispanic, socioeconomic status, and rural vs. urban.
Normative Data:	Originally based on 1,748 children from central Connecticut.

Title of Instrument:	Culture-Free Self-Esteem Inventories (J. Battle, 1981)
Source:	Special Child Publications
	6505 218th South West #13
	Mount Lake Terrace
	Seattle, Washington 98043
	(206) 771-5711
Purpose:	Assess self-esteem of children, adolescents, and adults (8 years to adult).
Length of Test:	About 20 minutes.
Reliability:	Test-retest = .81 for children; .82 for adults.
Validity:	Documented extensively. See instruction booklet for details.
Cultural Sensitivity:	The test is designed to be valid regardless of ethnic background.
Normative Data:	Normative data is provided, but only for the original sample group of 198. Later information on larger groups is scarce.

Title of Instrument:	Parenting Stress Index (Richard Abidin, 1983)
Source:	Pediatric Psychology Press
	320 Terrell Road West
	Charlottesville, Virginia 22901
	(804) 296-8211
Purpose:	Early identification screening, individual diagnostic assessment, and pretest-posttest measures of intervention effectiveness.
Length of Test:	120 single statement rating scale items.
Reliability:	Total Stress Score = .95.
Validity:	Documented extensively. See instruction booklet for details.
Cultural Sensitivity:	Cross-cultural validation is almost identical to the original test validity findings for the normative sample.
Normative Data:	Available for both mothers and fathers, but documentation for mothers is much more extensive.

(Continued)

Table 4.2

Descriptions of Standardized Outcome Instruments (Continued)

Title of Instrument:	Measurement of Meaning
Source:	C. E. Osgood, G. Suci, and P. Tannenbaum, *Measurement of Meaning*. Urbana: University of Illinois Press, 1957.
Purpose:	Community Assessment of Project: A set of rating scale items that can be adapted to any person, place, or thing to be rated. Find out the meaning of a community project to community members.
Length of Test:	100 items; 10-15 minutes.
Reliability:	Test-retest = .85.
Validity:	Depending on type of method used to measure validity, scores range from .72-.82.
Cultural Sensitivity:	No information.
Normative Data:	Not applicable.

Title of Instrument:	Anger Self-Report
Source:	Martin Zelin et al., Anger Self-Report: An Objective Questionnaire for the Measurement of Aggression. Journal of Consulting and Clinical Psychology, 39 (1972): 340
Purpose:	Measure anger for (1) awareness of anger; (2) expression of anger; (3) guilt; (4) condemnation of anger; and (5) mistrust.
Length of Test:	64 items.
Reliability:	Established for 138 subjects.
Validity:	Significant correlation found between scores on this instrument and other accepted measures with anger self-report components. Validated with 82 psychiatric patients and 67 college students.
Cultural Sensitivity:	No information.
Normative Data:	Provided for both normal subjects and psychiatric patients.

Title of Instrument:	Scales for Measuring Depression and Anxiety
Source:	C. G. Costello and A. L. Comrey, Scales for Measuring Depression and Anxiety. Journal of Psychology, 66 (1967): 303-313
Purpose:	Self-administered scale to determine degree of depression.
Length of Test:	21 items; minimal length of time to take test.
Reliability:	.90 for normal subjects; .82 for psychiatric sample with both high and low depression.
Validity:	Psychiatric clinical evaluations for psychiatric patients concurred with test results.
Cultural Sensitivity:	No information.
Normative Data:	240 normals: half male and half female; also available for psychiatric sample with high and low depression.

(Continued)

Table 4.2

Descriptions of Standardized Outcome Instruments (Continued)

Title of Instrument:	Piers-Harris Children's Self-Concept Scale (E. Piers, 1984)
Source:	Western Psychological Services
	Publishers and Distributors
	12031 Wilshire Boulevard
	Los Angeles, California 90025
	(213) 478-2061
Purpose:	Assess conscious self-concept in children and adolescents (8-18 years).
Length of Test:	About 20 minutes for an 80-item single statement self-report.
Reliability:	Test-retest ranges from .42-.96 for different samples.
Validity:	Documented extensively. See instruction booklet for details.
Cultural Sensitivity:	Research documentation for differences in scores is available for different groups, including Hispanics, Asian Americans, and Seminole Indians.
Normative Data:	Available for normal, learning disabled, emotionally disturbed, gifted, and other classifications of children and adolescents.

the difference is large enough to draw substantive implications. For example, if data from pretests and posttests indicate that the differences between these scores are statistically significant, but that posttest scores average only three points higher than pretest scores, what conclusions can be drawn from these results? The measure of statistical significance tells us the differences did not occur by chance. However, whether the differences are large enough to warrant a judgment that the program has been successful depends on the intent to which a few extra points is considered to achieve a meaningful level of change.

Normative test data may be a source of comparison if a standardized instrument that provides information about normative scores is used to gather the evaluation data. Normative data represent the expected distribution of scores based on the sample that was used to devise the instrument. The instructions that accompany a standardized instrument explain the expected scores for the test. If the sample used to develop normative data for the instrument is substantially different from the evaluation study sample, one must be cautious in the use of normative distribution of scores as evaluative criteria.

GROUP LEVEL OUTCOME EVALUATION
CASE EXAMPLES

Adolescent Support Group

A child abuse prevention agency serving an ethnic minority population has several programs for different segments of its target population. The programs include newsletters, crisis counseling, peer support groups for teenagers, and parent education workshops. The agency decided to evaluate the peer support group for teenagers that was offered in the junior high schools. The purpose of the service was to provide an opportunity for teenagers to talk about the bicultural issues and stresses that they face on a daily basis. The project sought to inform students about the nature of child abuse, child abuse laws and community resources, to foster communication and support among peers, and to instill cultural pride in the group participants.

Evaluation Question

The research questions were developed after the project's evaluation consultant observed one group of teenagers in the six-session support group program. The questions were (1) Does the program effectively convey information about child abuse? (2) Does the program help participants feel a sense of social support? (3) Does the program increase self-esteem?

Data Collection Instrument

The instrument developed consisted of three sections: (1) a question-and-answer sheet on child abuse information, (2) a social support inventory, and (3) the short version of Coopersmith's Self-Esteem Inventory. Pretesting the instrument with a group of potential clients resulted in its substantial modification.

Data Collection

Data were collected twice from each participant, once during the week immediately before the teenager started the program and once at the end of the last support session. For participants who were unable to attend the last session, attempts were made to contact those participants and to schedule a posttest within two weeks of the last session. Early in the data collection process it became clear that the amount of time required to complete the instrument (i.e., about 45 minutes) was too long. The agency reconsidered the decision to include the self-esteem inventory and decided to eliminate it. The decision was based on the need to shorten the test and on the fact that it seemed unlikely that significant gains in self-esteem would be attained through only six contacts with the project.

Data Analysis

The pretest scores were compared to posttest scores separately for the knowledge of child abuse information and for the social support inventory. A t test for paired data was conducted for each of the two variables by the evaluation consultant. The level of statistical significance was set at 0.05. The results of the t tests indicated that, while there was some improvement shown on the social support inventory on the posttest, it was not statistically significant. The improvement on knowledge of child abuse information, however, was significantly greater on the posttest.

Utilization of Findings

The agency decided to recommend elaboration of the support groups by increasing focus on social support opportunities and obstacles, and also by increasing the length of the program from six to eight weeks. These recommendations were based in part on the quantitative comparisons and in part on the answers to the items on the social support inventory. Those responses suggested that more time in the program might enhance the teenagers' ability to consolidate a social support network. The results and recommendations for program improvements were reported to the agency's funding sources and disseminated to all members of the staff.

Children's Street Theater

This project was a rural program combining theater classes and child abuse prevention for children 7-18 years of age. Theater classes were offered after school for children, and evening classes were available to both teens and adults. The method of instruction integrated theater games, play, and prevention. The students developed skits or revues about problems and solutions that related to child abuse and performed them for parents and peers. The project's goal was for students, while learning theater skills and working on the revues, to learn to trust themselves, learn to work within a group experience, develop a sense of self-worth, and educate their peers and community about the issues relating to child abuse prevention.

Evaluation Question

The project staff wanted to evaluate the experiences of participants and their parents to find out whether the program was effective and how the program was perceived by parents. A decision was made to focus on two specific questions: (1) Did the participants learn child abuse prevention concepts and information? (2) Did parents perceive the program as worthwhile and effective?

Data Collection Instrument

Program effectiveness was to be measured by changes in ability to answer questions about child abuse concepts. For the students, a small questionnaire was developed that consisted primarily of questions about prevention knowledge. For the parents, an open-ended survey was developed to provide a qualitative measure of any changes parents observed during the course of the program. Pretests and posttest were administered to two groups of students who participated in six weeks of theater classes. One group of students ranged in age from six to nine years; the other group from eight to eleven years. In addition, parents were surveyed once after the students' final performance for parents and peers.

Data Collection

Data were collected from the participants on the first day of the program and again on the last day of the program. In cases of absence, attempts were made to contact the participant and arrange a time to meet with them within one week of the originally scheduled session. Parents were surveyed immediately after the children put on their performance at the end of the six-week program. Parents who did not attend the final performance were not surveyed.

Data Analysis

For the six- to nine-year-old group, the overall change in scores from pretest to posttest was an 11% improvement. The change was not statistically significant at the 0.05 level. The eight- to eleven-year-olds demonstrated a 2% drop in scores from pretest to posttest, and again, the difference was not statistically significant. There are different possible interpretations for these findings. One possibility is that there was a poor fit between the program activities and the evaluation instrument. The instrument tested knowledge of prevention concepts, while the main content of the program seemed more focused on the related issues of self-worth, trust, and cooperation.

The results of the parent survey were more favorable. All of the parents surveyed indicated that they would have their child repeat the experience. When asked "How did this project help your child?" responses included: more self-confident, calmer, more outgoing, deals with problems and has learned to handle situations, more open and spontaneous, and has better self-image. The changes that parents would make were all along the same line of offering more classes and more public plays. The results of the parent survey were encouraging, but represented the views of only those parents who attended the final performance. It may be that parents who did not attend either disapproved of the program and did not want to support it, or were simply disinterested.

Utilization of Findings

Based on the findings, an evaluation consultant recommended that further research be conducted with a data collection instrument altered to reflect the issues that were addressed more directly by the program (i.e., self-worth, trust, and cooperation). Also, it was recommended that all parents be surveyed via telephone interviews during the week following the last performance, regardless of attendance.

Assault Survivor Support Group

This program provided centralized services for children who had been sexually assaulted out of the home and were 0-16 years of age, and their families. Services included 24 hour crisis intervention, follow-up, in-person counseling, advocacy, and group support. Project staff wanted to evaluate the sexual assault support group offered by the agency. The goals of the group were to increase self-awareness of feelings, beliefs, and behaviors resulting from sexual assault; to gain knowledge and the appropriate attitudes about sexual assault; to gain support from the group; and to increase self-esteem. Much of the curriculum was organized around the recognition and expression of feelings and building self-esteem.

Evaluation Question

Project staff elected to do an outcome study to ascertain their effectiveness in raising their clients' self-esteem. In addition, they wanted to determine if the clients learned a few critical attitudes and knowledge concepts that were introduced in the group.

A pretest-posttest design was used. The study sample consisted of five girls, their parents, and the primary clinicians rendering the services. Victims were administered a self-esteem measure before and after a ten-week group therapy program. In addition, one of the victim's parents, usually the mother, was also pretested and posttested about the victim's level of self-esteem. Finally, clinical observations were also made.

Data Collection Instrument

The project staff designated three instruments to measure the children's self-esteem, one for each set of respondents: victims, parents, and clinicians. The instrument used with the children was the Piers-Harris Children's Self-Concept Scale, a standardized 80-item, yes/no, self-esteem scale. A 22-item Likert-type scale was administered to the clients' parents. The scale was constructed from several of the variables listed on the Piers-Harris Children's Scale and was intended to elicit parents' perceptions, pre- and posttreatment, of their children's self-esteem. The clinical observations of the group leader, with respect to each child's self-esteem, were also recorded. In addition to the self-esteem measures, children's comprehension of the sexual assault information disseminated in the group was measured by a nine-item pretest and posttest of attitude and knowledge concepts. The instrument was constructed by the staff.

Data were collected from the children immediately before participation in the first session of the group therapy, and again on the last day of the group therapy. Data were collected from parents during the initial intake interview, and again after the last group therapy session. Clinical observations were collected throughout the ten-week program.

Data Analysis

During data collection, the clinicians noticed that there was a correspondence between parental perceptions of their children and the amount of change in self-esteem levels in the girls. The staff began to realize that they had little chance to improve on a child's self-image if the child was consistently getting negative messages at home. Nevertheless, the results for the pretest-posttest analysis for the five clients were positive. Although the sample size was too small to conduct statistical tests, the direction of change was positive and staff felt the amount of change was substantial.

Utilization of Findings

As a result of the pretest used, clinicians had a much better idea about the problems and effects of the assault and what to do to address those issues with individual clients. The correspondence between parental attitude and child self-esteem was addressed by modifying the program from a support group for the victims to a mother-daughter support group. Although the sample size placed limitations on the generalizability of the data to the study population, project staff were satisfied with the initial findings. They decided to offer the modified curriculum and to continue to collect data with the same instruments in order to generate a larger sample size.

Chapter 5

OUTCOME EVALUATION: CLIENT LEVEL

DEFINING THE EVALUATION QUESTION

Similar to group-level outcome evaluations, the assessment of client-level outcomes involves questions about how the target population is different after the delivery of services. There are, however, several special conditions associated with the client-level approach. First, it is required that the target population be made up of clients, either individuals or small groups such as couples or families, who are working with the agency over some period of time in order to make some personal changes. A primary prevention program that does public service announcements over the radio cannot evaluate its services with a client-level approach. In addition, one assumes that the types of changes sought by clients are tailored to their individual concerns. A judgment has been made that service goals are best defined according to the unique problems of each client at a given time. From a research perspective, this means that each client also has an individual set of evaluation questions based on their presenting problems. A client-level evaluation design provides a systematic approach to the collection of data on the achievement of individual service goals. These data may also be used to summarize client-level outcomes for the agency as a whole. The types of questions that are best addressed by client-level evaluation include:

- What percentage of clients who are receiving services at our agency reach their individual treatment goals?
- What are the problem areas most frequently found among our client population?
- For which types of problems do we most successfully meet treatment goals?
- For which types of problems do we least successfully meet treatment goals?
- Are certain programs within our agency more successful at meeting the treatment goals of clients than others?

Why Client-Level Evaluation in Child Abuse Prevention?

The child abuse prevention field is marked by diversity, at both the client and the provider level. Ecological models of causality for child abuse suggest that a wide range of interpersonal, socioeconomic, and sociological factors contribute to risk status. It follows then that clients of prevention programs vary widely in terms of demographic characteristics and with regard to the nature of presenting problems. Consequently, it is often difficult for a child abuse prevention agency to pose a singular measure regarding the effectiveness of its program.

Suppose, for example, the staff of a home-based parent support agency wanted to know if they helped their clients to be better parents. One of these clients is a refugee from Laos who has been labeled neglectful because her standards of parenting do not satisfy American norms. Another client is a native-born mother on AFDC who is stressed because her financial assistance does not cover the cost of living and she has no one to provide respite child care. The services provided for each mother will need to be quite different, and, although in both cases the problem areas addressed will help each mother to be a better parent, it would be inappropriate to assume that both mothers are working toward the same specific goals in the same manner. Thus, application of one standard of effectiveness would fail to capture important differences with respect to their situations, goals, and intervention experiences.

Just as clients represent a wide range of problems, providers vary with respect to the types of services they deliver and the treatment philosophies they bring to their work. A program to teach parents how to use contingencies to help control their children's behavioral problems involves a very different philosophy than that used by an insight-oriented therapist who tries to help the family understand feelings that the child is acting out with his or her behavior problems. Respite child care, parenting classes, counseling, and assertiveness training, are very different kinds of services, yet they can all be geared toward child abuse prevention. Often, a variety of services will be offered by one agency.

The point is, with all the diversity in clients, types of problems, services, and approaches to these problems, there are different ways to evaluate the outcomes of child abuse programs. This book will present one technique, called Goal Attainment Scaling, or GAS, that can be used to conduct a client-level outcome evaluation. It is a technique that allows for a great deal of individual flexibility and is also feasible to implement with limited resources. For these reasons, GAS is appropriate for use by a range of community-based child abuse prevention programs.

DEVELOPING THE EVALUATION STRATEGY

N=1 Design and Methods

Study designs for client-level evaluation are often referred to as n=1, or single-system designs. This is to distinguish them from group level designs where the "n," or sample size, is larger than one. All n=1 designs have some common characteristics.

- A target event, which can be a behavior, attitude, thought, or feeling, is identified.
- A system is devised for measuring the frequency of that target event in a consistent, valid fashion.
- The target event is measured at baseline, or before receiving services, and again after the intervention, and a comparison is made between the two time periods.

N=1 research differs from group-level research because the comparison is drawn between time periods for the same subject, rather than between groups. In the language of research, the client serves as his or her own control group. GAS is just one of many n=1 designs that can be used. Resources for information about other n=1 evaluation strategies can be found in the reference list at the end of the book.

An Overview of Goal Attainment Scaling

Goal Attainment Scaling was developed in the early 1960s by evaluators at the Hennepin County, Minnesota, Mental Health Service who were dissatisfied with existing ways to evaluate outcomes in mental health. They developed GAS as a measurement that would avoid both the inflexibility of standardized measures and the vagueness of unstructured observation, and would:

- allow for individualized problem definition;
- use each client as his or her own comparison in the measurement of success;
- allow for comparisons to be made of diverse treatment modalities (Kiresuk & Lund, 1978).

GAS involves the worker and client in identifying a number of mutually agreed upon problem areas. In each area a target goal is placed in the center of a five-point scale that represents the range of possible outcomes, from "most unfavorable outcome thought likely" to "best anticipated outcome." At intake, or in the assessment period, the client and worker construct the scales and document where the client is on each scale. The client's position on the scales is assessed again at an agreed upon follow-up date, or at the termination of services, after which time a follow-up score is calculated. The computation of the follow-up score, which will be explained in detail later, is an average of the scores on all of the client's individual goal attainment scales.

Translating Individual GAS Scores to Agency Evaluation

GAS can be thought of as a tool that allows a two-tiered evaluation. In the first tier, the evaluation focuses on the outcome of a specific intervention (or set of interventions) with respect to one client's goals. Since the goals are determined on an individualized basis, the evaluations can be very specific, flexible, and relevant. The evaluator is the practitioner, and the unit of analysis is the client. On the second tier, the evaluation focuses on the success of the program as a whole in meeting the treatment goals of its clients. Because the scales allow for a standardized method of scoring, they can be grouped together so that they are useful for making comparisons or assessing effectiveness of the program by aggregating the GAS scores of all of its clients. The evaluator is the program manager, and the unit of analysis is the

Table 5.1

Two-Tiered Model of GAS

- What percentage of clients achieve GAS follow-up scores of 50 or better?
- What are the problem areas most frequently found in our client population?
- In which problem areas do clients most frequently achieve GAS scores of 50 or better? below 50?

Manager will collect GAS
scores (or a sample) from all
workers and collapse them in
order to make assessments
about the program.

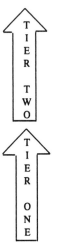

Worker will construct scales for
each problem area, and, at a
designated follow-up date, will
score each problem area and
calculate a GAS follow-up score.

Client Goals

- After 3 months of service, Ann will be able to demonstrate the correct use of "time out" as a nonabusive disciplinary strategy.
- While pregnant, Jane will feed herself at least two good meals a day.
- In the next four weeks, Lois will have applied for MediCal and AFDC for herself and her children.
- Mike and Terri will attend at least 8 out of 10 parenting classes at the community college.

---

program as a whole. As Table 5.1 illustrates, the research questions in each tier will be different, but interdependent.

The practitioner's individualized evaluation is not only a valuable clinical tool in and of itself, but it is also the foundation on which the manager's evaluation of the program as a whole rests. Since so much depends on the practitioner's implementation of GAS with each client, it is particularly crucial that the line staff support the evaluation endeavor. In order to avoid wasted effort and later disappointments, staff should be included in each stage of planning for this type of client-level evaluation.

At each tier, the evaluation question will need to be operationally defined. Perhaps the best way to illustrate an operationalized question at both tiers, and their interdependence, is to use a case example.

Case Example

Let's say that the administrator of a perinatal home visitor program wants to evaluate the effectiveness of her service. She chooses a client-level outcome evaluation strategy because of the population's wide range of problems and the workers' wide range of interventions. The global program evaluation question might be "Do our home visitor services help clients to achieve their goals?" The manager would generate an operational definition of that question by determining what observable, measurable indicator would let her know that clients were achieving their goals. GAS follow-up scores are her indicator of choice, and the subsequent specific operationalized program evaluation question might be "What percentage of clients who receive agency services for six months achieve GAS follow-up scores of 50 or better, indicating that, on average, they achieved the expected level of success toward their treatment goals?"

This administrator's successful implementation of an evaluation that will help her answer that question assumes that every home visitor is using goal attainment scaling and incorporating evaluation into the client work. The question that the practitioners will be asking is "Has my client achieved her specific treatment goal?" Let's say that the specific treatment goal is for client Ann K. to learn strategies to reduce her level of stress. An operational definition of Ann's goal might be if, after three months of home visits, Ann successfully used friends, family, or community resources for child care so that she could take breaks for at least two hours each week. This is a definition that includes a measurable, observable indicator that will tell the evaluator whether the goal of developing stress reduction strategies has been achieved. Developing operational definitions of treatment goals is at the core of GAS, and will be discussed in further detail in the section on data collection.

All of Ann K.'s treatment goals will be scaled and scored, and she will have a GAS score that indicates, on average, if she met her treatment goals in the program. The evaluator will collect the GAS scores of Ann K. and the other clients in the program, which will enable her to judge whether treatment goals are, on average, being met for the entire program.

Selecting the Study Population

Ideally, GAS will be used with all clients receiving the service being evaluated. Since GAS involves a change in the way that routine case documentation is done, a worker might avoid confusion by using it only with new intakes until, over time, the entire caseload has switched over. Easing in to GAS in this fashion also has the advantage of allowing the worker to learn the process with a small number of cases. Eventually, the practitioner will be evaluating every client, so that choosing a sample, or subset, of clients who will make up the study population is not a concern at this tier. At the agency tier it may be impractical in very large settings for an evaluator to use every case in the potential study population, and in this event a sample will need to be drawn.

COLLECTING THE DATA

Although we have discussed a general overview of how GAS works, up until this point the focus has largely been on its application as a client-level outcome evaluation tool at the agency tier. In the following sections, we will shift our focus to the worker/client tier and walk through the steps of actual data collection, that is, selecting a data collection instrument, assessing and choosing the problem areas to be addressed, constructing a goal scale, specifying a follow-up date, and finally scoring the goal scales.

Selecting the Instrument

Data collection tools can be either standardized instruments or ones that the agency devises on its own. The data collection instrument used in GAS is the Goal Attainment Follow-up Guide. Table 5.2 shows the basic follow-up guide format. It is a grid, with goal areas across the horizontal axis and scale values along the vertical axis. Of course, the basic format can be modified, and if another format for documenting goal areas and scales is more useful for any particular agency, then modifications should be made. Table 5.3, for example, is one agency's

Table 5.2

Goal Attainment Follow-up Guide

Name _____ Worker _____

Date For Initial Assessment _____

Date For Follow-up Assessment _____

Goal Areas / Outcome Scales Values	Weight (optional) _____	Weight (optional) _____	Weight (optional)
Most unfavorable outcome thought likely −2			
Less than expected success with treatment −1			
Expected level of success 0			
Better than expected success +1			
Best anticipated treatment success +2			

Table 5.3
Modified Goal Attainment Follow-Up Guide

pg._____of _____   SERVICE AGREEMENT

Name _____ Worker _____

Objective # _____

_____

_____

PLAN:

Parent(s) Tasks: _____

_____

Worker Tasks: _____

_____

Follow-Up Scale:

Intake Date:_____ Score_____ Follow-up Date_____ Score_____	Current behavior	Less than desired -2	Expected change 0	Best anticipated change +2

Objective # _____

_____

_____

PLAN:

Parent(s) Tasks: _____

_____

Worker Tasks: _____

_____

Follow-Up Scale:

Intake Date:_____ Score_____ Follow-up Date_____ Score_____	Current behavior	Less than desired -2	Expected change 0	Best anticipated change +2

modification of the grid format. They chose to use the modified data collection form because it was similar to the service agreement forms that were in use before the implementation of GAS, and was thus perceived to be less of an adjustment in documentation for the workers. Despite the slightly different layouts, each follow-up guide contains the basic components that allow the worker and client to specify the problem areas to be addressed, and provides at least three points on a scale of projected outcome measures.

Standardized, generic follow-up guide forms can be ordered from the Program Evaluation Project in Minneapolis, Minnesota. They have developed a series entitled *Guide to Goals*, which are instruction manuals offering technical assistance in the construction of follow-up guides.

Constructing the Follow-Up Guide

Identifying the Goal Areas

The first step in constructing the individualized evaluation instrument is to identify the goal areas. This process will not be unfamiliar to practitioners, who must routinely identify the presenting concerns of clients and make decisions about which of those will be selected as problems to be worked on in the course of treatment. Selecting goal areas for the purposes of evaluation is not too different. At this stage one shouldn't worry about specific outcome measures or progress indicators. The task is simply to choose, from the range of possible concerns, at least two, and no more than five, broad problem areas that will be the focus of work. Typical problems that come to child abuse prevention agencies are lack of child care, stress management, problematic child behavior, relationship conflicts, substance abuse, lack of resources, and so on. If there are more than five presenting concerns, it will be necessary to prioritize problems and choose those that are most important. When selecting the problem areas, practitioners can negotiate with clients to work first with those problems that meet as many of the following criteria as possible.

Guidelines for Prioritizing Problems
(Adapted from Bloom & Fischer, 1982; Gambrill, 1983)

- It is one that the client prefers to start with or about which they are most concerned.
- It is amenable to change.
- It is a problem that is appropriate for the agency and is a good fit with the workers' skills, that is, it is not the kind of problem that would be best handled by a referral out.
- It is a problem with a high danger value, meaning that it has a high chance of producing negative consequences if it is not handled.
- It has to be handled before other problems can be tackled. For example, working on marital communication is probably premature if one or both of the partners has an active drinking problem.
- Changes in the problem will result in tangible, observable changes for those involved, and may increase the client's motivation to work on other target problems.
- Client and worker *mutually* agree that it is an important problem area that is directly related to the client's needs.

Weighting the Goal Areas

The second step in constructing the Goal Attainment Follow-Up Guide is to weight each goal area to indicate its relative importance in comparison with the client's other problem areas. This is accomplished by assigning a number to each goal area that will be used in the calculation of the summary goal attainment score. The higher the number used in the weight, the more significant the goal area is, relative to the others. For example, if "alcohol abuse" seems twice as important as "finding day care" in the case of a particular client, the alcohol goal area might be given a weight of "2" and the day care goal area a weight of "1." The particular numbers chosen do not matter; it is the comparative, not the absolute, value of the number that is important for the purpose of weighting the goal areas. In the example above, if alcohol had been weighted "10," and day care "5," the final score would be the same. The same numbers should be given to problem areas that are judged to be equally significant.

In some cases, the evaluator may choose not to weight goal areas, treating all goals as though they are of equal importance. When goal areas are unweighted, calculation of the summary goal attainment score is simplified.

Operationalizing Goal Statements

After the problem areas have been selected and weighted, the next step is to transform the broad, vague problem categories into specific, measurable, and realistic goal statements that will serve as the center of the attainment scales.

For each problem area, a practical, specific progress indicator should be chosen that will be useful for assessing treatment outcome and can be efficiently, inexpensively, and reliably measured. Any problem area will have a variety of possible progress indicators. For example, if the problem area is alcohol abuse, one good progress indicator might be "number of drinks consumed per day," and another progress indicator for the same problem area could be "number of Alcoholics Anonymous meetings attended per week." Both indicators are appropriate to the problem area, measurable and specific.

Using the progress indicator selected as the measure of treatment outcome, the center of the scale, or the "expected level of success," is predicted. The expected outcome presents the most probable level of goal attainment that will have been reached by the date specified for the follow-up interview. The expectations ought to reflect what realistically "could" be attained given the individual strengths and limitations of the client and the time frame imposed by the follow-up date, rather than what "should" be attained.

With the "expected outcome" level completed as a benchmark, the four remaining outcome levels on the scale can be filled in. All levels on the scale for each problem area should use the same progress indicator, and only one should be used in each scale so that differential change along two or more dimensions will not make scoring impossible. The "expected level" of success should be the most probable outcome; the "most unfavorable" and the "best anticipated," the least probable outcomes; with probabilities for "better than expected" and "less than expected" outcomes falling somewhere in between.

When several goal areas have been identified and scaled, they should be reviewed for common errors that may make follow-up scoring problematic. The outcome predictions presented in the scales should be evaluated against the following Checklist for Reviewing Objectives.

Checklist for Reviewing Objectives
(Adapted from Gambrill, 1983)

1. Are clearly described: what, where, when, how often, who.
2. Are stated in positive rather than negative terms whenever possible.
3. Are attainable.
4. Are clearly related to the client's goal.
5. Focus on behaviors and/or environmental changes rather than on the indirect effects of change.
6. Confusion between outcome objectives (e.g., increase in parental praise for appropriate child behavior) and process objectives (e.g., attend parenting classes) is avoided.
7. If achieved, will modify the circumstances related to presenting concerns.
8. Build on client assets.
9. Progress will be easy to assess.
10. Outcomes are likely to be supported in real-life settings.

The final step in constructing the data collection instrument is to note the client's baseline, or current level of functioning, on the scales that have been created. This will enable the evaluator to derive at least two different kinds of effectiveness measures from the follow-up guide:

1. a GAS summary score that will indicate whether or not the "expected" levels of outcome are reached;
2. a GAS change score that will indicate whether or not change occurred.

Table 5.4 is an example of a completed GAS follow-up guide.

The Follow-Up Interview

When the scale is constructed, a time frame should be set based on agency policy and clinical considerations. For example, some programs are mandated to provide crisis services only, and can see clients for up to six weeks; in this case, the follow-up interview date would be set for no longer than six weeks after construction of the follow-up guide, or at termination of services if that occurs prior to the six-week limit. An agency that offers long-term treatment for survivors of abuse may use a longer time frame before follow-up, but could choose to score the follow-up guide in three-month intervals so that goals can be systematically reviewed on a regular basis throughout the treatment period.

Table 5.4

Goal Attainment Follow-Up Guide

Name __Any client__   Worker __Any worker__

Date For Initial Assessment __June 1__   *

Date For Follow-up Assessment __August 1__   4

Goal Areas / Outcome Scales Values	Anger Control Weight (optional) __8__	Child Care Weight (optional) __6__	Alcohol Abuse Weight (optional) 10
Most unfavorable outcome thought likely −2	Strikes, shakes, ignores when upset or screams because of child almost every day *	Can identify no resource for emergency child care except for this agency.	Attends one AA meeting and then refuses to attend. *
Less than expected success with treatment −1	Strikes, shakes, ignores when upset or screams because of child about 2X per week.	Can identify one friend or family member, and one community resource for child care, but does not plan for their use. ✔ *	Attends AA meetings sporadically. (Less than 4X per month)
Expected level of success 0	Strikes, shakes, ignores when upset or screams because of child about 1X per week. ✔	Has friends or family who provide at least 2 hours per week of respite care. Is on waiting list for regular child care.	Attends AA meeting 1X per week.
Better than expected success +1	Strikes, shakes, ignores when upset or screams because of child about 1X per month.		Attends AA meeting 1X per week and more often if necessary. ✔
Best anticipated treatment success +2	Does not strike, shake, ignore when upset or scream because of child at all.	Can identify at least 3 friends or family who could provide emergency child care. Children in child care program for regular respite 2X per week.	Attends AA meetings as necessary and asks spouse to attend Al-Anon.

Optimally, the predicted outcomes are selected with consideration to the time constraints.

At the specified follow-up date, the practitioner will determine where the client is with respect to the outcome scales, and will assign a "raw" GAS summary score. Using the completed follow-up guide in Table 5.4 as an example, we can see that asterisks indicate client status at intake, and check marks indicate client status at follow-up date. "Raw" scores at follow-up for each problem area are as follows:

Problem Area	Raw Score
Anger Control	−0
Child Care	−1
Alcohol Abuse	+1

These scores provide the basis for data analysis, which will be discussed in the following section.

ANALYZING THE DATA

Data analysis with GAS can be conceptualized according to two tiers in line with the evaluation question. On the first tier, the task of data analysis is to interpret scale scores for the individual client by generating a GAS summary score and a GAS change score. On the second tier, the summary scores for each client in the program are aggregated into a program statistic that indicates, on average, whether the agency was successful in meeting the treatment goals of its clients.

GAS Summary Score

The advantage of the GAS summary score is that a single number represents the findings from several diverse observations. The disadvantage is that the calculation of the score can be somewhat burdensome, particularly if the decision has been made to incorporate weighted scale areas. The summary scores produced have a theoretical range from 15 to 85 and typically form a normal distribution with a mean of 50 (Kiresuk & Garwick, 1975). A score of 50 indicates that a client has, on the average, exactly attained the "expected level of success" on his or her goals; a score of greater than 50 indicates "better than expected success"; and a score of less than 50 indicates "less than expected success."

Calculation with Weighted Scales

The formula used to derive the summary score incorporating weighted scales is

$$\text{Goal Attainment Score} = 50 + \frac{10 \times \Sigma \, w_i x_i}{(.7)(\Sigma \, w_i^2) + (.3)(\Sigma \, w^i)^2}$$

where w_i is the weight assigned to the ith goal scale, x_i is the "raw" attainment score (-2 to $+2$) on the ith goal scale of the GAS follow-up guide, and the summations are across all of the goal scales in the follow-up guide.

For those unfamiliar with mathematical notation, the formula can look intimidating, but it can be broken down into a series of relatively simple calculations that can be easily performed by anyone with basic math skills and the assistance of a calculator. Appendix 5.1, Calculating the GAS Summary Score, will provide a step-by-step breakdown of the mathematical operations necessary to complete the equation and yield a GAS summary score.

Calculation with Unweighted or Equally Weighted Scales

In cases where the scales have equal weights, or where scales are not weighted at all, the process is enormously simplified. In fact, in those cases Table 5.5 can be used to find the goal attainment summary scores. To do this, one must add the "raw" scale scores, find the row in Table 5.5 corresponding to this sum, and read the goal attainment score from the column corresponding to the number of scales in this follow-up guide. For example, if there were 4 problem area scales, and their outcome scores were 2, -1, 0, and 1, their sum is 2 and the goal attainment score is 57.

Using the Summary Score

After the summary score has been calculated, the practitioner has a number that indicates how closely the client has met treatment expectations. How can this number be used to provide meaningful feedback? A less than satisfactory GAS summary score should not necessarily be interpreted as failure. It is a piece of information which can be used:

Table 5.5

Goal Attainment Score Conversion Table for Equally Weighted Scales

Total raw score (Sum of scale scores)	Number of scales in follow up guide					
	1	2	3	4	5	6
-12						19
-11						22
-10					20	24
- 9					23	27
- 8				21	26	29
- 7				25	29	32
- 6			23	28	32	35
- 5			27	32	35	37
- 4		25	32	35	38	40
- 3		31	36	39	41	42
- 2	30	38	41	43	44	45
- 1	40	44	45	46	47	47
0	50	50	50	50	50	50
1	60	56	55	54	53	53
2	70	62	59	57	56	55
3		69	64	61	59	58
4		75	68	65	62	60
5			73	68	65	63
6			77	72	68	65
7				75	71	68
8				79	74	71
9					77	73
10					80	76
11						78
12						81

From Kiresuk & Lund, 1978

1. as a signal to modify the intervention if it is consistently ineffective with a particular type of problem or a particular type of client;
2. as a signal to reassess the level at which treatment goals are set (perhaps they are unrealistically ambitious and are setting the stage for inevitable failure); or
3. as a signal that more attention needs to be paid to the original assessment of client needs to ensure that the treatment goals selected are relevant and desirable to both practitioner and client.

Conversely, GAS summary scores that are consistently above expected success rates should not be cause for complacent self-congratulation. Certainly the positive feedback for work well done is important for both client and worker; however, when expectations are consistently exceeded, the practitioner might assess his or her level of goal setting to ensure that appropriately challenging treatment outcomes are sought.

GAS Change Score

A GAS change score indicates how much difference there is between baseline and follow-up. The score is determined by subtracting the GAS summary score calculated at the time the follow-up guide was constructed from the score calculated at the time of the follow-up interview. A negative score indicates regression; a score near zero indicates little or no change; a positive score indicates progress. A ten-point change indicates that a client has moved about one goal attainment level, as set up in the follow-up guide (Hagedorn et al., 1976).

Analyzing Agency Data

At the second tier of analysis, the scores from all the clients in the study population are collapsed so that the evaluator can generalize about the success of the agency as a whole. The most basic question that an analysis of GAS scores for the entire study population can answer is "What percentage of clients who are receiving services at our agency reach their individual treatment goals?" In order to answer this question, the evaluator must collect the individual GAS summary scores from all of the clients in the study population and do a simple tally to determine what percentage of those clients have GAS summary scores of 50 or better. In addition, it might be useful for the agency to know what the mean and median scores were, or how the program clients were distributed on the range of scores (i.e., the percentage of clients who had scores below 40, what percentage had scores of 40-60, and the percentage who had scores of 60 or better).

The GAS summary score can also be the basis for a comparative analysis, answering the question "Are certain programs within our agency more successful than others in meeting the treatment goals of their clients?" In this case, the study population would be separated into two groups of clients who received services from different programs within the agency. The mean GAS summary scores of the study populations could then be compared to tell the evaluator if one program was more successful than the other in meeting its client's treatment goals. A statistical test of significance could be applied to the two scores to determine if their difference was unlikely to have occurred by chance. If the scores were in fact different, the evaluator could conclude that one program was more successful than the other.

In this type of comparative analysis, it is important to remember that "success" is defined individually for each client so that there is nothing in the evaluation that ensures that the difficulties of the problem areas are comparable between groups. The evaluation determines if one program is more successful than another at meeting *its own* treatment goals, not if one is more successful than another in a universal sense.

PRETESTING THE EVALUATION METHOD

It is a good idea, particularly in those settings where the implementation of GAS as a research strategy is new, to pretest the evaluation method by subjecting a "pilot batch" of GAS follow-up guides to peer review. The practitioners at an agency might begin to implement GAS with a few cases that can be reviewed or audited by a peer group for the purposes of quality assurance. Issues that the group should attend to include:

- Problem areas selected for treatment should be appropriate for the agency.
- Scales should contain treatment expectations at an appropriate level of difficulty. Other practitioners working with a similar client population can provide good checks and balances in assuring that there is consistency throughout the agency with respect to level of difficulty.
- The group should agree that progress indicators chosen for particular problem areas are meaningful and provide a relevant measure of progress.

When follow-up interviews for the pilot batch of cases have been completed, the group can calculate the GAS summary scores and modify their construction of goal scales accordingly. If the first batch of scores is consistently low, perhaps that worker needs to construct more realistic goal scales. If the scores are consistently high, perhaps more challenging treatment expectations are required. The process of reviewing for these errors in a group and negotiating necessary corrections is an important one that ensures that workers are developing comparable treatment expectations so that, ultimately, scores will reflect differences in outcomes rather than differences in expectations.

A further benefit of using peer review as a standard method of ensuring quality assurance with GAS is that preferred methods of measuring frequently chosen goals will accumulate over time. These can be catalogued into a kind of scale library for the agency, which could serve as a reference. When common problem areas are selected as a focus of work with a new client, the practitioner can consult the library of previously constructed scales to see if they can be modified for use in the case, and avoid the time burden of reinventing the scales anew.

IDENTIFYING BARRIERS AND LIMITATIONS

There may be some unresolved questions about how useful and feasible client-level evaluation is. In an effort to anticipate some of those, we would like to mention a few commonly raised issues that are often raised as barriers to the implementation of Goal Attainment Scaling.

Barrier

"Doing evaluation with every client is just going to take too much time, and the workers are overloaded with paperwork as it is."

There is certainly truth to this objection. Although any agency, even those that are small and have limited resources, can do systematic self-evaluation, it would be misleading to pretend that it does not require a significant outlay of time and effort. Setting workable goals and constructing scales with clients are time-consuming, especially at the beginning when the process is unfamiliar. For this reason, it is important that the whole agency, administrative and direct service staff, supports the idea of incorporating evaluation into the work. This support must take the form of not only agreement on purposes and general encouragement, but also practical action such as reduced caseloads while workers are learning the process. After the learning period is over, the time burden should diminish, and it may be that the goal scales can actually reduce the time spent on paperwork if they can replace lengthy documentation techniques.

Barrier

"This technique sounds like it would work great for a behavior modification program, but that is not the treatment philosophy of my staff, so maybe it is not an evaluation technique that would work for us."

Behavioral practitioners have been the pioneers in much of single-system design research, but its use is not limited to that particular theoretical orientation. Remember for a moment the characteristics of single-system designs, including GAS.

1. A target event, which can be a behavior, attitude, thought, or feeling, is identified.
2. A system is devised for measuring the frequency of that target event in a consistent, valid fashion.
3. The target event is measured at baseline, or before receiving services, and again after the intervention, and a comparison is made between the two time periods.

Note that the target event does not need to be a behavior; it can be an attitude, a thought, or a feeling. It can be anything for which one can construct a measure. Furthermore, the design does not specify the type of intervention to be used, only that the target event will be assessed before and after intervention. Of course, in order to understand the results, one should clearly describe the intervention, but it certainly does not need to be a behavioral one. It might be insight-oriented psychotherapy, a parent's support group, or information and referral services. Many nonbehavioral practitioners have successfully used Goal Attainment Scaling.

Barrier

"I'm not a researcher, I'm a practitioner who responds to people's troubles. Doing all this evaluation stuff will get in the way of my work."

The goal of this research endeavor is to help practitioners in their work, not to get in the way. Insofar as evaluation helps to make systematic, informed decisions about interventions, we would argue that the research will help the work.

Barrier

"My clients are very crisis prone. I need to respond as emergencies occur, not stick to some set of goals that may no longer be relevant."

This can certainly be a problem in child abuse prevention agencies. Problems that occur in real life do not often fit the constraints of evaluation or intervention models that come out of books. If the agency is primarily one that delivers very time limited crisis intervention, than GAS may not be the evaluation strategy of choice. If, however, contact is maintained with clients for at least six weeks, then systematic goal setting and evaluation is possible. Needless to say, if a crisis comes up in midstream that is not a chosen goal area, the practitioner's responsibility is to respond to the crisis. As always, the worker's responsibility is to use his or her judgment and be willing to modify case plans as crises come up. Goal scales should not be adhered to rigidly in the case of an emergency. If one hopes, however, to be a planner as opposed to strictly a reactor, GAS can help structure case planning in order to accomplish this.

Presumably goals chosen before the crisis occurred will remain important, and may even contribute to the prevention of a subsequent crisis. When the immediate problem is resolved (e.g., the utilities are paid for with an emergency loan and heat is returned to the house; medical attention has been obtained for a sick family member), the previous work can resume.

If goals are chosen carefully and are viewed as meaningful by both the client and the worker, it is likely that they will continue to be relevant after the crisis has been resolved. If, however, the goals chosen become, for whatever reason, irrelevant, by all means renegotiate the goals. Again, the judgment is one that needs to be made by the worker, who is encouraged to respond with flexibility.

Limitation

"I understand the advantages of individualizing goals, but what about quality control? What if an agency fails at very ambitious goals, or succeeds at trivial or inconsequential ones?"

This observation points out a very real limitation. Goal attainment scaling provides the "what" and not the "so what" of evaluation. The evaluation results are only as meaningful as the goals. One way to minimize this limitation is to monitor the goals, especially in the beginning when workers are getting a feel for the process. One might review scores and goals after the first follow-up period; if scores are lower or higher than expected, check to see if goals are either too ambitious or not ambitious enough. There are no universal criteria; the appropriate range needs to be set for each agency. A periodic peer review session where goal scales are shared can help to ensure consistency between workers and monitor quality control.

Limitation

"I know enough about social science research to know that cause and effect is a very complex connection to make. Are you saying that monitoring progress toward treatment goals can prove that the changes are a result of my interventions?"

It is absolutely correct that establishing cause and effect requires more sophisticated research designs than goal attainment scaling. GAS can help determine whether or not desired changes have occurred without necessarily establishing the logical steps required to say that the changes are the direct result of the intervention. We maintain that monitoring for changes has a great deal of value, particularly for those programs that have resource restraints that do not allow for the costly endeavor of classical experimental research. If causality is a question of prime importance for you, however, please consider using more sophisticated experimental research designs.

CLIENT-LEVEL OUTCOME EVALUATION CASE EXAMPLE

Parent-Aide Program

This is a respite care and crisis intervention program in a moderately sized agricultural community. Client families are offered a service package that includes short-term respite child care, case management and referral, parent education classes, short-term counseling, and in-home visits to model parenting skills. All services are voluntary and short-term, about three months duration.

Agency Evaluation Proposal

The administrator wanted to focus self-evaluation efforts on the effectiveness of the in-home component of the program. Client families receiving in-home services were visited by a parent-aide who provided case management, crisis intervention, and parenting education through modeling. Recently, budget cuts had compelled the program to change its staffing pattern so that lay staff were employed as parent aides, a job formerly performed by professional counselors or social workers. The administrator was concerned about the staffing change, and her preliminary evaluation proposal was to determine how the program was impacting on its client families.

In the planning phases of the evaluation, meetings were held to solicit the opinions of the relevant program staff and incorporate their information needs into the evaluation design. The line workers were concerned that a uniform evaluation criterion would not capture the range of work that they did with a diverse, high-risk client population. In addition, the workers were anxious that the extra effort required to collect data would put further pressure on their already heavy schedules. In an attempt to allow the parent aides to address the wide range of client problems that occur in the target population, find an evaluation strategy that could be incorporated naturally into clinical work, and still have a measure suitable for evaluation purposes, this agency adopted Goal Attainment Scaling as an evaluation strategy.

Evaluation Question

At the individual level, the outcome evaluation question varied according to the specific presenting problems of each client. In each case, the general question could be stated as "Has the client achieved the expected level of success with respect to his or her individually negotiated treatment goals?"

At the agency level, the client-level outcome evaluation question was "How effective is the parent-aide program at meeting the treatment goals of its clients?" The operational definition of the question could be restated as "On average, do clients of the parent-aide program attain GAS summary scores that indicate that their treatment goals are being met?"

Study Design and Data Collection

The staff received training in the construction and scoring of evaluation scales, which were recorded on a standard GAS follow-up guide grid. A decision was made that practitioners would conduct follow-up interviews six weeks after intake, and again at termination of services. In those cases where termination occurred prior to the six-week interval, the follow-up interview was conducted at the time of termination. The time frame was chosen to allow for an assessment and possible renegotiation of treatment goals at the midpoint of services. On a regular basis (i.e., quarterly), the evaluation manager collected GAS scores for the study population from the parent aides.

Prior to the full-scale implementation of the evaluation strategy, workers were instructed to use GAS with a pilot sample of five clients each. Follow-up interviews were scheduled for six weeks after intake. The staff met as a group to review and score this first set of scales. In practice, the parent aides encountered several barriers that had made it difficult to implement the evaluation. First, they found that goal setting and scale construction took up more time than had been anticipated. Given the size of each worker's caseload, this extra time burden, despite its clinical utility, proved to be prohibitive. In addition, in those cases where initial attainment scores were constructed, the workers discovered that the first set of GAS summary scores was consistently low, averaging below 40, indicating that expectations had been systematically set higher than attainment.

Program management was supportive of the evaluation and allowed for several modifications suggested by the findings of the pretest. Caseload sizes were reduced so that the additional time involved in case planning and goal setting could be allocated. The conclusion drawn from the first set of scores was not that the staff was ineffective, but that they needed practice in setting realistic treatment goals with consideration to the time frame of follow-up, as well as the individual client situations. For the next few months, peer review meetings were scheduled on a regular basis, and scales were assessed for appropriate content and feasibility. At the next date established for follow-up interviews, the scores reflected a more even distribution, with some cases attaining expected treatment success, some exceeding it, and some falling below it. This led the administrator, who was assuming the role of evaluation manager, to feel confident that the "kinks" had been worked out of the data collection procedures and that, given regular peer review meetings to assure data quality maintenance, the strategy was feasible and valid for them. At this point, parent aides began to use GAS with all new intakes until, over time, it was being implemented with the entire service population.

Data Analysis and Utilization of Findings

In the first quarter that data analysis could be performed, the average score was 56, suggesting that, on average, client GAS scores reflected slightly better than expected treatment success.[1] Feeling confident that the peer review process was maintaining treatment goals at an appropriately challenging level, the administrator was able to conclude that the lay workers were providing services effectively, and that the treatment goals of clients in the home-visitor program were, on average, being successfully met. This evidence figured prominently in the agency's annual report to its funders, and informed subsequent decisions about the advisability of continuing to staff the parent-aide program with paraprofessionals.

NOTE

1. This is consistent with the study finding that paraprofessionals have generally been found to be as proficient as professional personnel in the construction of GAS follow-up guides as well as in the achievement of these goals through their work with clients (Kiresuk & Lund, 1978).

Appendix 5.1

CALCULATING THE GAS SUMMARY SCORE

Instructions for computing your GAS summary score:

1. Fill out the table on the following page with values from your GAS Follow-up Guide.

   a. In the first row, the "raw" score should be placed in the column corresponding to the goal scale.

   b. In the second row, place the weight value corresponding to the goal scale.

   c. In the third row, place the value obtained for the square of the weight, i.e., weight x weight.

   d. And in the final row, place the value obtained by multiplying the weight of the particular goal scale with its corresponding "raw" score.

2. In boxes A, B, and C, fill in the total obtained by adding the values in each row.

3. Find the square of the value in box C (C x C), and put that number in box D.

4. Multiply the value in box B by .7 (.7 x B), and place that number here in box E.

   ```
   | E _____ |
   ```

5. Multiply the value in box D by .3 (.3 x D), and place that number here in box F.

   ```
   | F _____ |
   ```

6. Add boxes E and F, and place that total here in box G.

   ```
   | G _____ |
   ```

7. Take the square root of box G, and place that number here in box H.

   ```
   | H _____ |
   ```

8. Multiply the number in box A by 10 (10 x A), and put that number here in box I.

I

9. Divide the number in box I by the number in box H, and put that number here in box J.

J

10. J + 50 = GAS summary score.

	GOAL #1	GOAL #2	GOAL #3	GOAL #4	GOAL #5	TOTALS	
SCORE (X)							
WEIGHT (X)						BOX C	BOX D
WEIGHT (X) WEIGHT (W^2)						BOX B	
WEIGHT (X) SCORE (W X)						BOX A	

$$\text{Goal Attainment Score} = 50 + \frac{10 \times A}{(.7 \times B) + (.3 \times D)}$$

Part II

COMMON TECHNICAL ELEMENTS OF PROGRAM EVALUATION

Chapter 6

RESEARCH DESIGNS

Research designs are usually categorized according to how they compare to the classic experimental design, which is the most rigorous scientific method for establishing proof. These designs fall into three basic categories: nonexperimental, quasi-experimental, and experimental. The various designs can be illustrated using the following symbols:

I   = Intervention
M   = Measurement
TG   = Treatment Group
CG   = Control Group
RTG = Randomly Assigned Treatment Group
RCG = Randomly Assigned Control Group

The symbolic representation of a one-shot case study, for example, is illustrated as TG: I/M. This means that the treatment group first experienced the intervention, then measurements were collected on that group.

NONEXPERIMENTAL DESIGNS

While the nonexperimental approach involves the least complex and least sophisticated research design, it is also the least costly in terms of time and money. These designs are characterized by the use of only one kind of control group, if any control is used at all. Consequently, they tend to be relatively weak with respect to establishing causality. There are three basic nonexperimental designs.

One-Shot Case Study
TG: I/M

In this, the weakest of the nonexperimental designs, a single group is studied only once, subsequent to a treatment or intervention intended to produce some positive change. For example, a process evaluation might entail surveying clients about a service delivery system after they received the services. Another instance would be one in which an observer monitors the services delivered on one occasion. For an outcome evaluation, a child abuse prevention program administrator might only need to know that parents leave the program practicing an adequate level of parenting. Generally speaking, this type of design is not highly recommended as there are no controls for extraneous factors, and it is therefore highly inferential and subject to misinterpretation. Under certain circumstances, however, such as programs that use a "one-shot" delivery technique that is uniquely formulated for a particular audience with whom there has been no prior contact (e.g., street theater, community education, and so on), this design may be all that is possible.

Pretest-Posttest Design
TG: M/I/M

This design involves assessments of a treatment group prior to and subsequent to the introduction of a program intervention. It is a stronger design than the one-shot study because the pretest measures provide a baseline against which to gauge change. Applied to a process study, this type of design is one in which clients are first surveyed about some aspect of the service delivery system; next, a change is made in the way the services are delivered; finally, the clients are surveyed again. The pretest-posttest design is often used to evaluate service outcomes. In trying to detect changes in clients' parenting practices, for example, parenting skills would be assessed before and after the program. If clients are not leaving the program with adequate parenting skills, or are not changing their parenting practices during the program, then further evaluation and/or program improvements are needed. If clients are observed to be practicing good parenting after the program as compared to their parenting practices before the program, then it is possible that the program contributed to this result. To increase the certainty of the program's effectiveness, however, more complex data collection strategies will be needed.

The pretest-posttest design addresses two important evaluation questions relating to causes of change: (1) Did the cause precede the supposed effect (e.g., are parenting scores higher after the program than before)? (2) Did the effect occur when the cause occurred? That is, did parenting skills improve when the program was in place? Any changes, however, in before-and-after measures found using the pretest-posttest design could conceivably be explained by influences other than program effects. Changes might have occurred simply because time passed and the program participants became more knowledgeable in general (e.g., parents demonstrated improved parenting skills because they had simply increased their parenting experiences). A popular television program might have been aired that addressed parenting skills. People who entered the program might have been more motivated to change, whereas less motivated people could either have ignored the program or dropped out during its early stages. Finally, pretesting could have sensitized group participants to the desired effects of the program and therefore precipitated any changes.

Static-Group Comparison
TG: I/M
CG: /M

This design represents a situation in which a group that has experienced the program is compared with one that has not for the purpose of establishing the effect of the intervention. This approach is stronger than the two mentioned above. It is the type of design that might be applied in a process evaluation of a therapeutic treatment program that has two types of cases. One set of cases originates from a referral source that has not been briefed on referral procedures; the other set of cases originates from a referral source that has received staff training (the intervention) on the agency's eligibility criteria, the referral process, and interagency coordination. Samples from both types of cases are taken for an audit to determine the appropriateness of the referrals, the efficiency of the referral process, and the interagency coordination. The results of both audits are noted and compared. If the results indicate a stronger performance by those who received the staff training, it is possible that the program contributed to the differences between the two groups. As with other nonexperimental designs, however, this design provides little control for the presence of other factors that may have influenced the results.

QUASI-EXPERIMENTAL DESIGNS

The principal difference between quasi-experimental designs and nonexperimental designs is that the former employ various experimental controls. Additional groups and/or additional tests may be used in a variety of combinations. These designs represent a compromise between nonexperimental designs, which do not really address the problem of external influences on the findings, and classic experimental designs, which seek to control for all external influence in order to clearly establish cause-and-effect relationships between the intervention and the results.

Additional experimental controls are needed in order to rule out alternative explanations for the findings. Some of the alternative explanations mentioned previously can be ruled out by combining a pretest-posttest design with the use of a comparison group, or pretesting half of the sample and posttesting the other half of the sample. These strategies can increase the certainty that observed changes are related to the program under study.

Pretest-Posttest Designs with Comparison Groups
TG: M/I/M
CG: M/ /M

A strategy for ruling out explanations for client change, other than program effects, is to monitor the progress of a comparison group that does not receive the program. As shown in Figure 6.1, both the treatment group and the comparison group are pretested and posttested, but only the treatment group experiences the program during the period under review. This design helps to rule out alternative explanations for client change. Also, the two groups should experience similar testing effects.

While this design can increase certainty regarding program effects, a major weakness in it has to do with the lack of control over the characteristics of the treatment and comparison groups. If the two groups are not similar, any differences in their results could be attributable to the initial differences in their characteristics rather than the

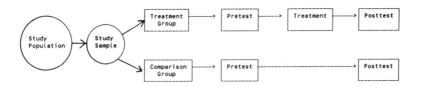

Figure 6.1
Pretest–Posttest Design With Comparison Group

program under evaluation. Therefore, it is necessary to assess the degree of similarity between the treatment group and comparison group on the key variables of interest. Since it is often the case that a program will have a greater number of referrals than can immediately be served, clients assigned to the waiting list can be used as a comparison group. This is true as long as the waiting list reflects a "first-come, first-served policy," rather than a priority assignment based on client characteristics. This strategy avoids many of the ethical dilemmas associated with withholding services.

The two groups should be matched on basic demographic variables, such as sex, ethnicity, age of parents, age of children, level of education, and so on. For example, if the program under evaluation targets change in specific areas such as expanding knowledge of child development or improving household management skills, it would be a good idea to match the functioning of the two groups for any of those areas that were of interest. If the comparison group appears to be similar in all or most of the variables measured, then some guarded generalizations about the effectiveness of the program on clients with these types of characteristics can be made.

Split-Half Designs
TG1:   /I/M
TG2: M/I/
CG1:   / /M
CG2: M/ /

If data are collected both before and after the program, participants may anticipate the "correct" answers to the questions on the posttest because of their experience during the pretest. This effect is particularly

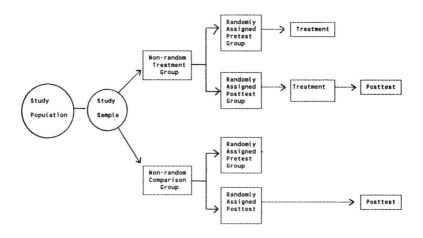

Figure 6.2
Split-Half Design

problematic when the variables to be measured reflect changes in attitude or personal behaviors (e.g., response to stress, attitude toward corporal punishment) rather than more objective conditions (e.g., household income, level of welfare benefits, residence in substandard housing). One way to avoid this "test bias" is to conduct the pretest with only half of both the treatment and control groups, and administer the posttests to the other half of both groups at termination. If these group members are randomly assigned to receive either the pretest or posttest, then the difference in the average pretest and posttest scores can be considered to represent the average gains generated by the service program. A diagram of this design is shown in Figure 6.2.

Improvements in each of the above separate strategies can be achieved by combining them. Treatment and comparison groups could be split into halves for pretesting and posttesting over repeated time intervals. The two groups would not experience test bias, and useful comparisons could be made over time.

CLASSIC EXPERIMENTAL DESIGNS

While there are several possible refinements of the experimental design, the basic form of an experimental design is to randomly assign members drawn from randomly selected samples to either a treatment

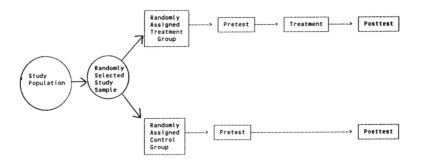

Figure 6.3
Basic Experimental Design

group or a control group. Thereafter, all treatment and control groups are treated identically, except that the control group(s) does not receive the program service.

Basic Experimental Design
RTG: M/I/M
RCG: M/ /M

In its basic form, the classic experimental design involves a single pretest-posttest strategy. The treatment group(s) would follow this schedule: (1) pretest at a given time before the program; (2) receive the program; and (3) posttest at a specified time after the program. The control group(s) would experience only steps 1 and 3 with the same amount of time elapsing between tests as the treatment group experienced. This design is diagrammed in Figure 6.3.

Long-Term Follow-Up

If an evaluation of the program's long-term impact is needed, then posttest groups can be contacted again at a later date. There are difficulties, however, in finding clients after a long period of time. One strategy for tracking clients is to use, with the client's consent, administrative records such as AFDC payment records or motor vehicle records. An alternative is to give clients that will be contacted later a self-addressed postcard with which to notify the agency of a change of address.

Given the difficulty in finding clients, most follow-up studies tend to base their conclusions on data from those clients most available or agreeable to postprogram interviews. Such a sample, while more convenient than tracking a random sample, runs the risk of being biased since programs often have more success in tracking less mobile, more stable, or more cooperative former clients, or in interviewing a disproportionate number of clients who had a positive program experience. Since these clients do not represent everyone in the program, they may yield results that overstate a program's success.

The extent to which client groups being studied represent the population of clients from which they are drawn depends upon the manner in which these groups are selected. The methods commonly used to select a proportion of the client population as research subjects includes both random and nonrandom techniques.

SAMPLING TECHNIQUES

Random Sampling Techniques

Systematic Random Sampling

In systematic random sampling, a sampling rate (e.g., one out of every four clients) is established. The actual selection (whether to select the first, second, third, or fourth client in each group of four) is randomly determined.

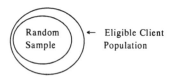

To select a systematic random sample, follow these steps:

1. Define the population of clients you intend to study (e.g., single mothers, the general population, all families who have been reported for child abuse).
2. Make a list of that population. If it is premature to do that, decide how all the eligible participants will be identified as they appear (e.g., participants as they arrive for the presentation, phone book).
3. Decide on a sample size (no less than 30).

4. Decide the proportion of the total population that the designated sample represents. For example, if you choose a sample of 40 and you usually have 200 single mothers in your program, then the proportion is 1/5.

5. Once this ratio is determined, you know the rate at which to select your sample. Decide which of the first five names on your list you're going to start. You can do this by drawing numbers out of a hat.

6. Pick every fifth name following the first choice until the desired sample size is achieved.

7. *Remember:* You can only generalize the results of your evaluation to the original population you defined in Step 1.

Scenarios appropriate for systematic random sampling are:

- A test is administered to every fifth person who viewed a movie on child abuse.
- An audit is done on every fifth client record in the file drawer.
- A list of clients is drawn up according to when they entered a program. Every fourth one is requested to complete a client satisfaction survey.

Stratified Random Sampling

In stratified random sampling, the client population to which the

findings will be generalized is divided into subsets. The variables used to define these subsets depend on the differences among clients that are of interest and likely to affect the findings. Once divided into subsets, a client sample is then randomly selected from each subset.

To select a stratified random sample, follow these steps:

1. Identify the major characteristics of interest in the study population. Certain descriptive characteristics that distinguish one group from another might be chosen, for example, sex, age, ethnicity, knowledge, attitudes, services site, caseworker, and variables of interest.

2. Sort the population into subpopulations according to the variables selected (e.g., number of single mothers, number of unemployed single mothers, number of clients receiving services from staff member A).

3. On the basis of the relative proportions of the subpopulation, select randomly if possible, a sample of people from the subpopulation in accordance with your desired sample size. For example, if you plan to select a total sample of 100 and you know that 10% of the population are Hispanic, one-parent families, then select 10 people from Hispanic, one-parent families to be in the sample.

4. Repeat this process of selecting desired strata of the community according to their proportions in the community until you have a total, representative, stratified sample.

Scenarios appropriate for stratified random sampling are:

- Relative consistency of service delivery between various staff members is determined by sorting clients according to workers. Client files are randomly selected within these groupings.
- Service effectiveness with diverse ethnic groups is established by sorting clients into groups according to the features to be compared. Clients are randomly selected from these groups for inclusion in the evaluation.
- Adequacy of service delivery throughout multiple sites is determined by listing sites and then randomly selecting clients to survey at those sites.

Nonrandom Sampling Techniques

Nonrandom sampling is a method of choosing a portion or sample of a population in such a way that not every element in the population has an equal chance of being included in the resulting sample. Evaluators select nonrandom samples for a variety of reasons. Sometimes they are not in the position to select a random sample; sometimes they consciously choose to do a nonrandom sample.

The primary reasons for selecting a nonrandom sample are that it is impossible to choose a random sample because of problems that limit access to clients served; a random sample may take too long given the time allotted to do the evaluation; a random sample is too expensive; and the evaluator makes a conscious decision to examine a hand-picked sample because, for example, of the need to audit certain cases that have come to attention as being problematic to serve. Three of the major types of nonrandom sampling designs are:

Convenience Sampling

The sample is chosen by using whatever elements or subjects are available.

Scenario: You are under the gun to produce this evaluation, which was due yesterday. You have three presentations scheduled for the next two weeks and you intend to use the recipients of these presentations in your sample.

Quota Sampling

The sample is selected by dividing the population into different strata and hand picking a proportion of elements from each strata.

Scenario: You want to review the work of all four of your staff. You make a list of recently closed cases for each one of your staff. You select five of the most recently closed cases of each of your staff to audit.

Purposive Sampling

The sample is chosen based on the judgment of the researcher that these elements are typical of the population.

Scenario: You select a particular school to sample in evaluating the quality of your service delivery system based on your belief that the racial and socioeconomic make up of the subjects are typical of the population you serve.

DATA COLLECTION PLANNING

Once decisions are made about the research design and sampling techniques, the evaluator's attention turns to the tasks of scheduling the collection of data and training data collectors. Establishing an evaluation schedule involves working from global data collection time frames to specific timelines that correspond to the distinct data collection activities. Initially it involves looking at the overall evaluation design and determining how the various aspects of this design affect the timing of research activities. Then it is a matter of plugging in the sequential activities and the corresponding numbers to arrive at the specifics.

Consideration needs to be given to the following factors:

- the deadline for the evaluation study;
- the deadline for data collection given the completion date for the overall study;
- the total sample size needed;
- conditions surrounding the nature of the sample that affect the timing of data collection; for example, access to school children and school teachers is subject to the school schedule; access to individual clients is dependent on their entry into the system;
- conditions surrounding the use of the selected methodology that affect the timing of data collection; for example, observation of a primary prevention program has to coincide with the schedule of presentations; surveys given to respondents will be administered to clients at the end of each parenting class during their 12-week session;
- conditions surrounding the specifications of the study design that affect the timing of the data collection; for example, pretests have to be administered to clients during the intake phase; posttests are administered to clients upon termination of the service; and follow-up interviews must be scheduled sometime after the clients complete a program;
- the amount of time in which one can reasonably expect to obtain the sample of cases required;
- the number of data collectors that are available to collect the data.

Data Collection Tools

There are a variety of tools for planning data collection. They differ in purpose, content, scope, and organization, reflecting the diversity of planning needs and foci. Three planning tools are presented here as useful guides for scheduling data collection. A close examination of these tools reveals that, although they have elements in common, they serve very different purposes.

The first tool, the Information Collection Plan (ICP), Table 6.1, was developed by Fink and Kosecoff (1978). It is organized according to specific data collection techniques used in an evaluation. This approach is most useful in conceptualizing the data collection process. The following steps outline how Fink & Kosecoff intend the ICP to be used.

Step 1:   Name each separate data collection technique.

Table 6.1
Information Collection Plan

Specific Information Collection Techniques (Instruments)	Time and Place for Information Collection	Nature of the Sample for the Technique	Who Will Collect the Information
Pencil and paper knowledge test	One week before and one week after presentation	All participating 3rd grade students in 3 schools	Evaluation Team Data Collectors
Interview with teachers	One week after presentation	Teachers of participating 3rd graders in 3 schools	Evaluation Team Data Collectors
Interview with parents	Days 2 and 3 after presentation	Parents of participating 3rd graders in 3 schools	Evaluation Team Data Collectors
Interview with children	One week before and one week after presentation	Randomly selected 3rd grade students in 3 schools	Evaluation Team Data Collectors

Step 2: Evaluator records when and where each instrument will be administered, to whom and by whom. Will some information collection methods be used more than once? How long will it take to complete the activity? Where will the information collection take place? All these points should be included on the ICP.

Step 3: Evaluator must record on the ICP whether information will be collected from all participants or only some. If only some individuals are going to be sampled, they should be identified.

Step 4. The evaluator should record on the ICP who will collect the information (i.e., external evaluators).

The next tool, Table 6.2, is a modified Gantt chart. Gantt charts are used to plan and control complex sequences of activities necessary for the completion of a project or task. These charts may appear dramatically different; however, the one characteristic they all have in common is the sequential and temporal listing of essential tasks. In the sample Gantt chart, data collection activities have been listed sequentially and

Table 6.2
Modified Gantt Chart

Study Areas and Tasks 10/7/88	Main Responsibility	Doers	Staff Days	Week # 1	Week # 2	Week # 3	Week # 4
SCHOOL #1							
Classroom # 1							
Parent Letters	NG	MR	1	X			
Child Pretest	NG	LF	1	X			
Parent Interview	NG	MR	2	X			
Teacher Interview	NG	MR	1	X			
Child Posttest	NG	MR	1		X		
Classroom # 2							
Parent Letters	NG	MR	1	X			
Child Pretest	NG	LF	1	X			
Parent Interview	NG	TM	2	X			
Teacher Interview	NG	TM	1	X			
Child Posttest	NG	TM	1	X	X		
SCHOOL #2							
Classroom # 1							
Parent Letters	JP	MR	1		X		
Child Pretest	JP	LF	1			X	
Parent Interview	JP	MR	2			X	
Teacher Interview	JP	MR	1			X	
Child Posttest	JP	MR	1				X
Classroom # 2							
Parent Letters	JP	MR	1		X		
Child Pretest	JP	LF	1			X	
Parent Interview	JP	TM	2			X	
Teacher Interview	JP	TM	1			X	
Child Posttest	JP	TM	1				X

temporally, tasks have been assigned to staff, and completion dates have been determined. This type of format is useful for staffing and scheduling the data collection.

The third tool, Table 6.3, is a sample schedule of the data collection phase. The data collection activities are listed sequentially by date. The block spacing allows one to view a week of tasks at a glance. The

Table 6.3
Schedule of Data Collection for All Schools

Place	Measure	Date	Staff
Olympia	Teacher Pretest	9/12/87	M
Olympia	Parent Pretest	9/14/87	K
Lakeview	Teacher Pretest	9/15/87	M
Lakeview	Parent Pretest	9/17/87	K
Olympia	Teacher Presentation	9/21/87	M
Olympia	Child Pretest	9/22/87	M/H/K
Olympia	Parent Presentation	"	K
Lakeview	Teacher Presentation	9/23/87	M
Lakeview	Child Pretest	9/25/87	M/H/K
Lakeview	Parent Presentation	"	K
Olympia	Child Presentation	9/28/87	M/H
Lakeview	Child Presentation	9/30/87	M/H
Fording	Teacher Pretest	9/31/87	M
Fording	Parent Pretest	"	K
Fording	Teacher Presentation	10/5/87	M
Fording	Parent Presentation	10/7/87	K
Fording	Child Pretest	"	M/H/K
Fording	Child Presentation	10/13/87	M/H
Olympia	Teacher Posttest	10/18/87	M
Olympia	Parent Posttest	10/19/87	K
Lakeview	Teacher Posttest	10/20/87	M
Lakeview	Parent Posttest	"	K
Olympia	Child Posttest	10/26/87	M/H/K
Lakeview	Child Posttest	10/28/87	M/H/K
Fording	Teacher Posttest	11/2/87	M
Fording	Parent Posttest	11/3/87	K
Fording	Child Posttest	11/9/87	M/H/K

schedule provides a system that ensures that every data collection activity at the multiple evaluation sites will be accomplished in proper order and in timely fashion. It also provides a list of staff assignments, eliminating confusion regarding who is doing what.

TRAINING DATA COLLECTORS

In planning for the data collection process it is important to bear in mind that data collectors often require some form of training. Ideally, trainees should be given a context within which to place their research activities. This helps to clarify what it is they are doing and the information being sought. Also, it serves to boost morale. If the data collectors are unfamiliar with the program, they should receive a brief orientation in order to grasp the relationship between service activities and the overall objectives of the study. Finally, they should learn about the data collection instruments and tasks.

Training Session

Trainees should be given detailed instructions on how to obtain and record the data. The elements of a good training program include:

- a review of the general data collection guidelines and procedures;
- a review of the data collection instruments and related materials;
- practice in administering the instruments;
- practice in recording data;
- instructions on handling potential problems.

It is helpful for trainees to receive a packet of materials relevant to the data collection that would remain in their possession. This packet includes:

- copies of data collection instruments and forms;
- directions for administering instruments and collecting data;
- list of possible problems and sample solutions;
- names, addresses, and phone numbers of contacts and locations of data collection;
- names and phone numbers of evaluation team to contact in case of difficulties or questions.

The training session can be divided into segments that incorporate the components identified above. It can be conceived of in the following way:

Review of General Guidelines and Procedures

It is advisable to review general operating procedures and expectations with the data collector trainees. This provides an opportunity to
cover topics such as appropriate dress, establishing a rapport with
respondents, recording responses exactly as stated, and having a working familiarity with the data collection instruments.

Review of Data Collection Instrument and Related Materials

It is recommended procedure to review the data collection instrument, item by item, as a group. Each item should be read aloud, its
purpose elucidated, and questions about it discussed with the group. It
is also useful to review procedures about how to handle difficult or
confusing situations that may occur in response to items in the instrument.

Role-Play of Data Collection

Perhaps the most effective technique for training data collectors is
to participate in and observe role-playing of the data collection process.
The trainer can alternate playing the roles of data collector and respondent for purposes of demonstration. Acting as the respondent, the trainer
can set up problems that the trainee might encounter. The observers in
the group can practice recording responses from the role-play. The
group can then compare their responses. Following the demonstration,
trainees can be paired off to practice on each other, alternating roles.

Review of Initial Data

Regardless of whether or not the first three to five interviews are part
of the actual sample, it is a good idea for data collectors to meet with
trainers and review the data gathered in these initial efforts. Here the
trainer examines the data for evidence of misunderstanding and clears
up any confusion that may appear. In some cases, the trainer may want
to reconvene the entire group after their initial data collection efforts to
share experiences, rekindle confidence, and infuse new enthusiasm.

Chapter 7

DATA COLLECTION INSTRUMENTS

This chapter examines how to construct instruments for the systematic collection of data. Several key issues on assessing instrument quality are explored, and strategies for testing an instrument to ensure that it is ready for use are presented.

DEVELOPING DATA COLLECTION INSTRUMENTS

In this section, we analyze the construction of data collection instruments and offer guidelines for developing instruments related to four methods: audits, surveys, observations, and tests.

Audit Instruments

Developing an audit instrument requires creating one or more checklists. The checklists cover the aspects of a program to be evaluated (e.g., service delivery process, inputs to the program) and address questions concerning the quality and appropriateness of the services delivered. Each item on the checklist is compared to the relevant best practice standards and correspondence (or lack of correspondence) is recorded. Table 7.1 shows an excerpt of an audit checklist for service provision with sources for the practice standards in parentheses.

Table 7.1

Excerpt of an Audit Checklist for Service Provision Case Planning

---

Circle One:

Yes	No	Are outside consultants used in difficult cases? (BPA, 1977)
Yes	No	Is the initial case service plan completed within 90 days of the initial application or referral? (Peat et al., 1978)
Yes	No	Are treatment goals realistic outcome statements? (BPA, 1977)
Yes	No	Are treatment goals measurable outcome statements? (BPA, 1977)
Yes	No	Are treatment goals unambiguously defined? (BPA, 1977)
Yes	No	Are service plans based on utilization of agency and community resources? (Peat et al., 1978)
Yes	No	Do treatment plans specify the services to be offered as well as who will provide them? (BPA, 1977)
Yes	No	Are the service goals geared to the parent's ability to achieve them? (Peat et al., 1978)
Yes	No	Are the service goals made clear to the family? (Peat et al., 1978)

Survey Instruments

Data collection instruments for client surveys solicit information through a series of open-ended (e.g., What did you think of our program?) or fixed-choice (e.g., rating scales, multiple choice) questions. Table 7.2 gives examples of these different types of questions. The major disadvantages of open-ended questions are the coding and analysis difficulties that arise when generalizations are being developed from a sample of written responses. These questions, however, offer respondents an opportunity to express their views in greater depth and variety than fixed-choice questions permit. While fixed-choice questions limit possible responses, they can be constructed so that a broad range of alternative views is listed. In addition, fixed-choice questions do not present coding and analysis problems.

It is often desirable to use more than one type of question in a survey. For example, respondents may first be asked to rate whether they think that the program content is appropriate, and then to explain their response. This combination of fixed-choice and open-ended questions often benefits the data analysis: The ratings are relatively easy to use to summarize the data and the open-ended comments take more effort to analyze, but ultimately will permit better explanations of the ratings

Table 7.2

Question Types for Survey Instruments

Examples of Open-Ended Questions

- How useful do you find respite care?
- What are the biggest problems that come up for your family?
- What does your family do well?
- What is a "good" parent?

Examples of Fixed-Choice Questions

Multiple Choice

1. If I feel like hitting my child, I

   a. have no one to help me.

   b. know about places in the community where I can go.

   c. feel that it's a private matter that I will deal with alone.

2. If I see someone abusing a child, I usually

   a. mind my own business.

   b. try to stop them.

   c. have guilty feelings about it.

Rating Scales

Child abuse is best prevented by creating severe penalties for perpetrators.	Agree	1	2	3	4	5	Disagree
It is better to keep the family together after an incident of child abuse than to take the child out of the home.	Agree	1	2	3	4	5	Disagree

---

provided by respondents. Table 7.3 shows an excerpt of an actual survey form with both fixed-choice items and an open-ended item.

In the following tables, a variety of guidelines are provided for the construction of survey instruments. Table 7.4 reviews the steps to take in developing a survey instrument. Table 7.5 lists specific hints and criteria for construction of self-administered surveys. Table 7.6 lists specific hints and criteria for construction of an interview survey.

Table 7.3

Excerpt from a Parenting Workshop Consumer Satisfaction Survey

Program Evaluation Form

In order to make our workshops more effective, we need your help. Please answer the following questions as honestly as you can. All answers are strictly confidential, and it is not necessary to write your name on this sheet.

1. How do you feel about the workshop so far?

____ Very Pleased   ____ Somewhat Pleased   ____ Very Disappointed

____ Somewhat Disappointed   ____ Not Sure Yet

2. Please rate the teaching methods used so far:

	Not Very Useful	Somewhat Useful	Very Useful	Not Sure Yet
a. Lectures	____	____	____	____
b. Demonstrations of technique	____	____	____	____
c. Role-playing	____	____	____	____
d. Discussion	____	____	____	____
e. Handout Materials	____	____	____	____

Comments _____

_____

_____

3. Please rate the subject matter covered so far:

	Not Very Useful	Somewhat Useful	Very Useful	Not Sure Yet
a. Roles and responsibilities	____	____	____	____
b. Communication skills	____	____	____	____
c. Handling family conflict	____	____	____	____

4. If you have seen actual positive changes at home since you started the program, please describe:

_____

_____

_____

_____

_____

SOURCE: Adapted from Austin et al., 1982.

Table 7.4

Steps for Construction of a Survey Instrument

1. Specify the survey method that will be employed (e.g., written questionnaire, face-to-face interview, telephone interview).
2. Identify the questions that are appropriate for the specific variables that will be used in the evaluation.
3. Specify the type(s) of questions that will be used and determine the formats (e.g., if a rating scale will be used, define the points on the scale).
4. Review the checklist that is pertinent to the project: Table 7.5 contains instructions for the construction of written surveys, and Table 7.6 lists instructions for surveys conducted by interviewers.
5. Write questions for the instrument.
6. Group the questions according to thematic content.
7. Within thematic groupings, group questions according to type of answer required (e.g., list together questions that are answered with the same rating scale).
8. Write clear, explicit instructions for the respondent or interviewer throughout the instrument, especially when new subsections are introduced.
9. Using the guidelines provided in Tables 7.5 or 7.6, check the instrument for clarity, accuracy, redundancy, and length of time it takes to complete the questions.
10. Pretest and assess the quality of the instrument using the tests provided later in the chapter for quality assessment and pretesting.

Interview surveys are similar to self-administered surveys, but have additional instructions for the interviewer.

Observation Instrument

Items on observation instruments range from numerative categories (e.g., number of times child smiled) to forced-choice questions (i.e., those specifying categories such as Yes/No) to open-ended questions (e.g., What kinds of attitudes were displayed?). These various types of observations permit the collection of both quantitative and qualitative data. In designing these instruments, each variable should be carefully assessed with regard to the format that will be most effective for recording observations of that variable. An example of an observation instrument dealing with a trainer/teacher's style of presentation is illustrated in Table 7.7. This instrument provides forced-choice items with opportunities for open-ended comments.

Table 7.5

Guidelines for Construction of a Self-Administered Survey

PRINCIPLES

DO ask only those questions that serve the purpose of the survey.

DO ask only those questions that call for information that respondents can be expected to know.

DON'T ask personal questions (e.g., income, intimate behavior) unless it is necessary.

DON'T use names of persons or institutions that may bias answers.

LENGTH

DO design the questionnaire so that it can be completed in about 15 minutes.

FORMAT

DON'T squeeze all of the questions together compactly on the questionnaire in an attempt to use as few pages as possible. It causes respondents to miss questions, to misinterpret questions, and to feel overwhelmed.

DO maximize the white space on your questionnaire. Spread out the questions so that each page is uncluttered. The layout of the questionnaire should be clear and attractive.

DON'T use open blank spaces for respondents to check their answers. If respondents are sloppy, it will be difficult to interpret the intended responses.

DO use boxes (produced by right and left brackets or parentheses) that can be checked or response numbers or words that can be circled.

DO make the forms user-friendly by numbering pages and inserting phrases such as (Over) and (Continued).

DON'T assume that respondents will automatically know how to complete the questionnaire.

DO include introductory comments and clear instructions on *every* questionnaire.

DO provide respondents with basic instructions for completing the questionnaire. Tell them exactly how and where to indicate their answers.

DO make known whether an item requires a single answer or multiple answers by clearly indicating such options in the instructions.

DO use headings in the questionnaire if certain questions can be grouped into content subsections.

DO consider using a standard set of response categories (e.g., very satisfied, somewhat satisfied, neutral, somewhat dissatisfied, very dissatisfied).

DO preface content subsections with a short statement concerning their content and purpose.

DO arrange the layout, when asking close-ended questions, so that all answers are in a column separate from the questions. It will be easier to tabulate answers.

(Continued)

Table 7.5
Guidelines for Construction of a Self-Administered Survey (Continued)

QUESTION CONSTRUCTION

DO   consider the average comprehension level of the survey group when preparing the introduction and questions. Use the simplest language possible.

DO   consider the use of open-ended questions in order to probe into the thinking or views of the respondents. Be aware, however, that there is an unlimited range of responses that may prove hard to analyze and code.

DO   consider fixed-choice questions when it is clear what specific questions to ask and the range of likely responses is known. All possible choices must be available.

DO   consider using rating scales in which a set of close-ended response categories (e.g., very satisfied, satisfied, neutral, and so on) are used in answering questions, because of the advantages afforded the evaluator, the staff, and the respondents in terms of efficiency.

DO   name all of the response categories instead of merely the two end points on a rating scale. Each point on the scale needs to be defined so that respondents and agency staff have a mutual definition of the unit.

DON'T   exceed four or five units on a rating scale. There is no consensus regarding use of an even number or an odd number of rating points.

DON'T   use double-barreled questions that require the respondent to give one answer to a two-pronged question (e.g., Were the content and length of the presentation appropriate?).

DO   break a complex idea into two or more questions. Include only one point in each question.

DON'T   use double negatives (e.g., he didn't dislike . . .). Use the positive phrasing instead.

DON'T   use unfamiliar abbreviations, initials, or acronyms.

DO   use words that have the same meaning for everyone. Some words or phrases have different interpretations. Define terms that may be ambiguous.

DON'T   use general, vague, or unspecified terms (e.g., often, many, usually). Make questions concise, clear, and unambiguous.

DO   minimize wordiness in questionnaire questions and responses.

DO   be specific when asking questions about frequency or quantity (e.g., do *not* ask "Do you often scold your child?" Ask "Do you scold your child more than seven times a week?")

DO   state questions neutrally in order not to present a biased point of view.

SEQUENCE

DO   be aware that the ordering of the questions can influence the answers. Respondents strive for consistency in their responses.

DO   alternate statements representing different orientations so that respondents do not pick up a pattern and begin answering thoughtlessly.

(Continued)

Table 7.5

Guidelines for Construction of a Self-Administered Survey (Continued)

SEQUENCE (Continued)

DO begin the questionnaire with the most interesting, albeit nonthreatening, set of questions to pique the interest of the respondents. Place duller, demographic information at the end of the questionnaire.

DO place questions in logical order for the respondent.

DO have the simple questions precede complex, thought-provoking, or time-consuming questions.

DO present general questions before specific ones.

DO have open-ended questions precede close-ended ones, when appropriate.

DO pose less sensitive inquiries before more sensitive questions.

DO place questions in succession of decreasing importance on the survey.

DON'T use more than one set of standardized response categories or reverse the order of a rating scale from one question to the next. Respondents may become confused and inadvertently provide incorrect responses.

Ratings and short answers take less time to record, are easier to analyze, allow the observer opportunities to focus on the phenomena under review, and help ensure that different observers will provide comparable data. Open-ended comments, on the other hand, may be more difficult to analyze and compare, but they permit the recording of relevant data that may not be anticipated.

Prior to and during construction of the observation instrument, it is helpful to record observations in a mock session. Taking the time to conduct an observation session before beginning construction of the instrument is a sound investment. In this phase, the observer is instructed to record observations freely, without any checklist items or questions. Analysis of the data obtained from this experiment often provides practical information and new insights on how to focus the instrument and record data. Table 7.8 lists the steps to take to construct an observation data collection instrument.

Inter-Rater Reliability

One of the most challenging aspects of constructing an observation instrument is to ensure consistency from one observer to the next. When data from different observers are examined for consistency, the assessment is referred to as *inter-rater reliability,* or inter-coder reliability.

Table 7.6
Guidelines for Construction of an Interview Survey

PRINCIPLES

DO   ask only those questions that serve the purpose of the survey.

DO   anticipate the respondent's point of view. She or he doesn't know what to expect or anticipate about the content of the interview. Be patient.

DO   ask only those questions that call for information that respondents can be expected to know. People often guess if they don't know the answer.

DON'T   ask personal questions (e.g., income, intimate behavior) unless it is necessary.

DON'T   use names of persons or institutions that may bias answers.

DO   have interviewers record respondents' replies to open-ended questions exactly as given, because interviewers will not know how the responses are to be coded before the processing of the data.

DON'T   allow interviewers to summarize, paraphrase, or correct the bad grammar of a respondent in their written records.

DO   have the interviewers add comments in the margin related to the respondent's demeanor, gestures, or tone, especially where the respondent's actual verbal response was vague or inarticulate.

LENGTH

DO   design the face-to-face interview so that it can be concluded in less than 30 minutes in a home setting and less than 5 minutes on the street.

DO   design a telephone interview so that it can be completed in less than 15 minutes.

FORMAT

DON'T   squeeze all of the questions together compactly on the questionnaire in an attempt to use as few pages as possible. It causes interviewers to miss questions.

DO   type questions along the narrow dimension of the paper, allowing adequate space for replies.

DO   type questions only on one side of the paper.

DO   arrange the layout, when asking close-ended questions, so that all answers are in a column separate from the questions. It will be easier to tabulate answers.

DO   use boxes (produced by right and left brackets or parentheses) that can be checked or response numbers or words that can be circled.

DO   make the forms user-friendly by numbering pages and inserting phrases, such as (Over) and (Continued)

DO   provide interviewers with basic instructions for completing the questionnaire. Tell them exactly how and where to indicate their answers.

(Continued)

Table 7.6

Guidelines for Construction of an Interview Survey (Continued)

FORMAT (Continued)

DO make known whether an item requires a single answer or multiple answers by clearly indicating such options in the instructions.

DO use headings in the questionnaire if certain questions can be grouped into content subsections.

DO consider using a standard set of response categories (e.g., very satisfied, somewhat satisfied, neutral, somewhat dissatisfied, very dissatisfied).

DO preface content subsections with a short statement concerning their content and purpose.

QUESTION CONSTRUCTION

DO consider the average comprehension level of the survey group when preparing the introduction and questions. Use the simplest language possible.

DO consider using open-ended questions in the first draft of the survey in order to identify the range of possible answers to offer for future fixed-choice questions.

DO consider fixed-choice questions when it is clear what specific questions to ask and the range of likely responses is known. All possible choices must be available.

DO consider using rating scales in which a set of close-ended response categories (e.g., very satisfied, satisfied, neutral, and so on) are used in answering questions, because of the advantages afforded the evaluator, the staff, and the respondents in terms of efficiency.

DO name all of the response categories instead of merely the two end points on a rating scale. Each point on the scale needs to be defined so that respondents and agency staff have a mutual definition of the unit.

DON'T exceed four or five units on a rating scale. There is no consensus regarding use of an even number or an odd number of rating points.

DON'T use double-barreled questions that require the respondent to give one answer to a two-pronged question (e.g., Were the content and length of the presentation appropriate?).

DO break a complex idea into two or more questions. Include only one point in each question.

DON'T use double negatives (e.g., he didn't dislike . . .). Use the positive phrasing instead.

DON'T use unfamiliar abbreviations, initials, or acronyms.

DO use words that have the same meaning for everyone. Some words or phrases have different interpretations. Define terms that may be ambiguous.

DON'T use general, vague, or unspecified terms (e.g., often, many, usually). Make questions concise, clear, and unambiguous.

(Continued)

Table 7.6

Guidelines for Construction of an Interview Survey (Continued)

QUESTION CONSTRUCTION (Continued)

DO   be specific when asking questions about frequency or quantity (e.g., do *not* ask "Do you often scold your child?" Ask "Do you scold your child more than seven times a week?")

DO   state questions neutrally in order not to present a biased point of view.

SEQUENCE

DO   orient the respondent to the focus of the interview by providing a brief introduction to it.

DO   place screening questions at the beginning to establish whether the respondent is eligible to answer the question.

DO   be aware that the ordering of the questions can influence the answers. Respondents strive for consistency in their responses.

DO   alternate statements representing different orientations so that respondents do not pick up a pattern and begin answering thoughtlessly.

DO   start the questionnaire with a simple, nonthreatening question to establish a rapport with the respondent.

DON'T   start off the interview with a question that will put the respondent on the defensive.

DO   place questions in logical order for the respondent.

DO   have the simple questions precede complex, thought-provoking, or time-consuming questions.

DO   present general questions before specific ones.

DO   pose less sensitive inquiries before more sensitive questions.

DO   place questions in succession of decreasing importance on the survey.

Inter-rater reliability should also be checked immediately prior to collection of data after all other pretests and revisions have been made. The steps to take in assessing inter-rater reliability are:

- Have all observers make independent observations of the same observation session. (This can be done for a live session, but using a videotaped session will allow for later clarification of disagreements.)

- Ask the observers to respond to the items on the observation instrument while observing the session.

- After all observers have completed the observation session and filled out the instrument, tally the number of agreements for all fixed-choice items.

Table 7.7
Excerpt of an Observation Checklist

Voice Qualities		Comments
1. Volume	_____ appropriate	
	_____ too loud	
	_____ too soft	
	_____ too monotonous	_____
2. Tone	_____ appropriate	
	_____ dull	
	_____ too excited	_____
3. Pitch	_____ appropriate	
	_____ too high	
	_____ too low	
	_____ too monotonous	_____
4. Clarity	_____ clear	
	_____ mumbles	
	_____ slurs	
	_____ too clipped (difficult to follow)	_____
Conversation		
1. Length of statements	_____ appropriate	
	_____ too brief	
	_____ too long	_____
2. Humor	_____ appropriate use	
	_____ too little (too serious)	
	_____ too much	
	_____ inappropriate timing	_____
3. Feedback	_____ appropriate listener feedback	
	_____ too little	
	_____ too much	
	_____ inaccurate	
	_____ too critical	
	_____ unvarying	_____

SOURCE: Adapted from Trower, P., Bryant, B., and Argyle, M., 1978

Table 7.8

Steps for Construction of an Observation Instrument

---

1. Identify the questions that are appropriate for the specific variables that will be used in the evaluation.

2. Specify the type(s) of questions that will be used and determine the formats (e.g., if a rating scale will be used, define the points on the scale).

3. Review the checklist presented in Table 7.9 for the construction of observation instruments.

4. Write out the items for the instrument in the manner in which the observer should respond to them.

5. Organize the items according to the order most relevant for your study (e.g., thematic grouping, ratings, chronological developments).

6. Write clear, explicit instructions to the observer throughout the subsections of the instrument.

7. Return to the guidelines provided in Table 7.9, and check the instrument for clarity, accuracy, redundancy, and amount of time it takes to complete the questions.

8. Pretest and assess the quality of the instrument using the test provided below and those provided later in this chapter for pretest and revision.

- Inter-rater reliability is calculated by dividing the total number of possible agreements by the total number of coded agreements. That number is then converted to a percentage by multiplying by 100.

$$\frac{Total\,number\,of\,agreements}{Total\,number\,of\,possible\,agreements} \times 100$$

The guidelines presented in Table 7.9 are applicable to all forms of observation instruments.

Testing Instruments

Development of tests to measure clients' knowledge, skills, changes in attitude, and so on, can be a challenging task. Tests aimed at assessing change in relatively abstract phenomena, such as attitudes and self-awareness, are often complex and require time, effort, special populations, and expertise that normally are beyond the scope of self-evaluation research. Thus, for some topics, such as parenting attitudes or self-esteem, it is practical to select an instrument that has been developed and tested by researchers with experience in these areas. Tests of knowledge are easier to construct and to tailor to specific programs. A data collection instrument to test for knowledge generally contains a

Table 7.9

Guidelines for the Construction of a Direct Observation Recording Form

---

GENERAL PRINCIPLES

DO develop a recording form that permits easy, accurate collection of information. One of the primary reasons for inaccurate and incomplete data is a failure to provide an easy recording procedure.

DO devise a recording form that will be appropriate for the conditions surrounding the observation and the nature of the information to be collected.

DO determine whether the observer should merely note the occurrence of an event/behavior, note the frequency of the occurrence, subjectively rate the event or behavior, or do some combination of the above. These decisions will dictate the type of recording instrument to be constructed.

DO prepare standard recording forms in advance of the observations if it is known ahead of time that specific behaviors, actions, or events will be recorded.

DO use specially designed forms to make recording easier. This could be a checklist, a rating form, a grid for recording the frequency or occurrence of events or behaviors, or any other format that will facilitate the recording.

DON'T let advanced preparation or standard forms limit or stifle the observation or recording. Record unanticipated observations as well as expected observations.

DO consider a combination of recording styles where appropriate and useful (e.g., narrative recording and checklist on the same instrument).

DO consider developing a symbolic shorthand or coding to speed up recording.

GENERAL FORMAT

DO make certain that the layout is attractive.

DO provide ample space for the observer to use in recording observations.

DO pay attention to special needs for information. Provide spaces for the date, service location, and other identifying information.

DO make the forms user-friendly by numbering pages and by inserting phrases such as (Over) and (Continued).

DO include instructions and introductory comments on every recording form about how to complete the form (i.e., how and where observers should indicate answers or note their observations).

GENERAL RECORDING PROCEDURES

DO record observations while observing, whenever possible, for maximum accuracy.

DO write down the observations as soon as possible after making the observations if on-site recording is not possible.

DON'T trust to memory.

DO take notes as unobtrusively as possible. People are likely to alter their behavior if they see an observer taking down everything that they say or do.

(Continued)

Table 7.9

Guidelines for the Construction of a Direct Observation Recording Form

(Continued)

SPECIALIZED RECORDING FORMS

DO label both axes of any grids used on the instrument.

DO arrange the layout on forms such as checklists so that all answers are in a column separate from the questions. It will be easier to tabulate the answers.

DO consider coding and computer entry needs when designing the questionnaire forms.

DO make certain that recording forms are organized and not cluttered or confusing.

NARRATIVE RECORDING PROCEDURES

DO consider a narrative recording format that is unstructured and free form if a running account of the sequence of events and behaviors is needed.

DO record first the most important observations.

DO record things, if there is sufficient time, that may not seem important at the outset. They may turn out to be more important, or they may trigger something that is relevant.

DO include both empirical observations (i.e., descriptions of what is actually seen) and interpretations of observations (e.g., opinions, elaborations, explanations) in the notes. Empirical observations should, however, take precedence over interpretations, since interpretations can be formulated retrospectively if the evidence has been recorded.

DON'T record inferences in place of behavior.

DO make certain that any inferences made are clarified by identifying the concrete observations.

DO record empirical observations separately from interpretations of observations.

DO take notes on observations in stages. In the first stage, be as sketchy as necessary. In the second stage, rewrite the notes in detail.

DO rewrite any notes as soon as possible after making the observations.

DON'T put off rewriting the notes, even overnight. Rewrite while the recollections are fresh in your memory.

DO write out all the details that can be recalled when rewriting the observations, because it won't be possible to distinguish important from unimportant details until all of the data collected have been reviewed and analyzed.

---

series of open-ended or fixed-choice questions. Table 7.10 shows examples of question types for a testing instrument.

It is usually advisable to use more than one type of question on a test. A combination of fixed-choice and essay questions can provide rich

Table 7.10

Question Types for Testing Instruments

Examples of Open-Ended Questions

1. What discipline strategies do you use with your child?
2. How would you define a "good touch"?
3. What is a "good" parent?

Examples of Fixed-Choice Questions

True/False

   1. T   F   A spanking that leaves bruises is not child abuse.

   2. T   F   It is okay to talk to a stranger if that stranger knows the password.

Multiple Choice

   Child abuse is

     incest.
     beating your child.
     leaving your young child unattended for a long time.
     all of the above.

Rating Scales

   1. I spank my child

always	often	sometimes	rarely	never

   2. I use a time-out discipline

always	often	sometimes	rarely	never

---

information. If respondents answer fixed-choice questions incorrectly (or correctly), it will be possible to summarize their performance easily, but it may not be at all obvious why certain items were answered in certain ways. If a few open-ended questions are included, the respondents' knowledge may be tapped in such a way that it will be possible to explain the results of the tests. For example, a series of multiple-choice questions about parenting strategies could be followed

Table 7.11

Steps for Construction of a Test Instrument

1. Identify the questions that are appropriate for each of the specific variables to be studied.
2. Specify the type(s) of questions that will be used and determine the formats (e.g., true/false, short answer).
3. Write questions for the instrument.
4. Arrange the order of the questions so that there is a random pattern for correct answers.
5. Write clear, explicit instructions for the respondent and/or administrator.
6. Using the guidelines provided in Table 7.12, check the instrument for clarity, accuracy, redundancy, and length of time it takes to complete the questions.
7. Pretest and assess the instrument using the tests provided in the section on pretesting and revision that are relevant.

by an open-ended question about strategies used in the home and why they are used.

Table 7.11 lists the steps to take to construct a test instrument. Table 7.12 provides a list of guidelines for the construction of a test instrument.

ASSESSING INSTRUMENT QUALITY

Validity, reliability, and cultural sensitivity are important concerns in judging the quality of a data collection instrument. Validity has to do with the relevance of the instrument's content. It addresses the question "Does this data collection instrument really measure what it is supposed to measure?" For example, to test for parenting skills, if subjects are asked about their knowledge of discipline strategies, will that indicate whether their skills have actually improved?

Reliability has to do with the consistency of scores with repeated use of an instrument. Does the instrument measure attitudes, knowledge, and/or behavior in the same way each time it is used? Data collection instruments that most clearly demonstrate the problem of reliability are those used with observational techniques. If observer A uses an observation instrument to assess family interactions via videotape, will she or he obtain the same results as observer B, using the same instrument

Table 7.12
Guidelines for Test Construction

PRINCIPLES

DO ask only those questions that serve the purpose of the test.

DO ask only those questions that call for the information that respondents can be expected to know.

DON'T ask personal questions (e.g., income, intimate behavior) unless it is necessary.

FORMAT

DON'T squeeze all of the questions together compactly on the test in an attempt to use as few pages as possible. It causes interviewers to miss questions, to misinterpret questions, and to feel overwhelmed.

DO maximize the white space on the test instrument. Spread out the questions so that each page is uncluttered. The layout of the test should be clear and attractive.

DON'T use open blank spaces for respondents to check their answers. If respondents are sloppy, it will be difficult to interpret the intended responses.

DO use boxes (produced by right and left brackets or parentheses) that can be checked or response numbers or words that can be circled.

DO make the forms user-friendly by numbering pages and inserting phrases such as (Over) and (Continued).

DON'T assume that respondent will automatically know how to fill out the test.

DO include introductory comments and clear instructions on *every* test.

DO provide respondents with basic instructions for completing the test. Tell them exactly how and where to indicate their answers.

DO make known whether an item requires a single answer or multiple answers by clearly indicating such options in the instructions.

DO arrange the layout, when asking close-ended questions, so that all answers are in a column separate from the questions. It will be easier to tabulate answers.

QUESTION CONSTRUCTION

DO consider the use of open-ended questions in order to probe into the thinking or views of the respondents. Be aware, however, that there is an unlimited range of responses that may prove hard to analyze and code.

DON'T use double-barreled questions that require the respondent to give one answer to a two-pronged question (e.g., Yes No Is it okay to spank a child if there are no marks left or if there are bruises?).

DO break a complex idea into two or more questions. Include only one point in each question.

DON'T use double negatives (e.g., he didn't dislike . . .). Use the positive phrasing instead.

(Continued)

Table 7.12
Guidelines for Test Construction (Continued)

QUESTION CONSTRUCTION (Continued)

DON'T   use unfamiliar abbreviations, initials, or acronyms.

  DO   use words that have the same meaning for everyone. Some words or phrases have different interpretations. Define terms that may be ambiguous.

DON'T   use general, vague, or unspecified terms (e.g., often, many, usually). Make questions concise, clear, and unambiguous.

  DO   minimize wordiness in test questions and responses.

  DO   state questions neutrally in order not to give away the answer.

SEQUENCE

  DO   be aware that the ordering of the questions can influence the answers. Respondents strive for consistency in their responses.

  DO   randomize the pattern of correct answers so that respondents do not pick up a pattern and begin answering thoughtlessly.

DON'T   use more than one set of standardized response categories or reverse the order of a rating scale from one question to the next. Respondents may become confused and inadvertently provide incorrect responses.

---

with the same videotape? If both observers are adequately trained and their results are different, the instrument is not reliable.

Cultural sensitivity has to do with the appropriateness of an instrument for different cultural groups. Is the instrument based on values that are applicable to different ethnic groups? Do the concepts presented in the instrument "translate" in the same manner to members of the different ethnic groups in the client population? This is a particularly important consideration when more than one ethnic group is represented in the client population. Information regarding the reliability and validity of existing instruments varies; data on the cultural sensitivity of instruments usually are not available.

The tests for reliability, validity, and cultural sensitivity that are provided below should be used if:

- the data collection instrument will be constructed specifically for a given evaluation study;
- the data collection instrument is a standardized measure that will be modified for a given evaluation study;

their children. In addition to child abuse prevention concepts, they were queried as to their attendance at the recent parent training and their previous training. Responses were numbered in such a way as to produce raw scores, which provided the respondents with feedback on their level of knowledge on the topic. The results, shown in Figure 8.3, indicate that parents who had recent training or previous training had more knowledge of child abuse prevention concepts than those who had no training.

Frequency Distribution: Example 3, Histogram. Figure 8.3 is called a histogram because it is a specific type of graph that involves grouping the data into manageable categories. If parents' individual test scores had been graphed, the figure would have been unreadable (and extremely tedious to draw!). In cases where there are too many different data points, and logical/numerical categories can be determined, grouping them together can clarify the information.

Inferential Statistics

It is common in evaluation research to compare the results from two or more groups. A study sample may be both pretested and posttested, for example, with the finding of interest being whether there is any real difference in the before and after scores. It is also typical to compare the performance of two different groups (e.g., the performance of adolescent parents and adult parents on a parenting skills inventory). The problem that arises when comparing such scores is how to know when a difference in scores between groups, or from pretest to posttest, really reflects a difference that can be attributed to some outside influence (such as the program), or whether the difference in scores is simply a matter of chance. Under normal circumstances, the scores obtained on a given day from a given group can reasonably be expected to change at least a little bit. *The trick is to know when the difference is not due to some chance variation but actually reflects a systematic change in the sample.* For example, if 100 clients took a parenting inventory before and after a parenting skills course, and their mean scores were 70% correct before the program and 80% after the program, would such a difference be sufficiently large to warrant a claim about the merits of the program? In this case, in order to support a claim about the effects of the program, the evaluator might want to conduct a statistical test to compare the scores of the two groups.

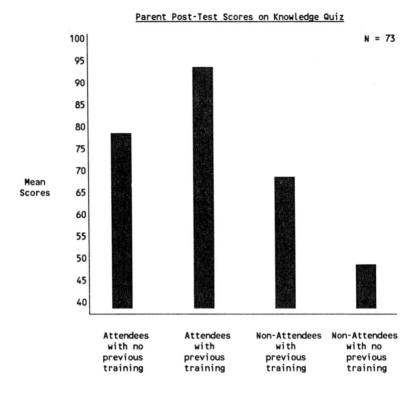

Figure 8.3
Example of Histogram

Inferential statistics are a set of mathematical techniques designed to evaluate the relationships between groups of data. The following description of basic concepts and statistical tests is provided in order to assist the evaluator in determining the types of analyses that are possible and the types of data that must be collected in order to use specific techniques. The discussion of these techniques in this manual is not comprehensive nor exhaustive; rather, it is intended to provide the reader with a general familiarity with the types of issues that are relevant when conducting statistical analyses. For complex analyses, it is necessary to consult an expert. For simpler applications, however, the information provided in this section, when combined with a good statistics textbook and a calculator (or, preferably, a good statistics textbook, a statistical package for computers, and a computer) may be sufficient for an enterprising evaluator to conduct in-house statistical analyses.[1]

In order to understand how inferential statistical tests can be used, it is necessary to become familiar with a number of basic concepts. These include:

* type of measurement
* type of distribution
* level of statistical significance
* assumptions about the data
* sample size

Type of Measurement

The choice of a specific statistical test depends in part on the types of variables that are used. Variables may be either categorical or numerical in nature. Within these two groups, there are further distinctions. The basic classification system most commonly used distinguishes between nominal and ordinal measurement for categorical variables, and between interval and ratio measurement for numerical variables.

Nominal measurements are qualitative categories and do not have any inherent ordering relationships between each other. Gender, place of birth, religion, and ethnic group are all examples of nominal variables.

Ordinal measurements are categorical data that can be rank-ordered according to some quantitative criterion, although the distance between the categories remains undefined. The hierarchy of agency personnel is an example of an ordinal scale. Management, line staff, and clerical support positions reflect a type of higher to lower ordering. Another example is that of class status in our culture. A simplified order in this case is upper income, middle income, and lower income. Finally, the classification of the severity of personal problems experienced by an agency's clientele represents an ordinal scale. Clients may be grouped according to whether their problems are very severe, severe, moderate, and so on. In each of these examples, note that, although there is a logical rank-order to the categories, it is not possible to quantify how far it is from one category to the next. One could not specify, for example, the "distance" from moderate problems to severe problems.

Interval measurements have both consistent ordering and consistent distance relationships. An interval measurement is any numerically ordered system where the distance between any two consecutive points is equal to the distance between any other two consecutive points. The Fahrenheit (F) temperature scale is an example of an interval scale since the distance between 72°F and 73°F, for instance, is the same as that between 99°F and 100°F.

Another characteristic of interval measurements is that the place on the scale for zero is arbitrary. When there is only an arbitrary position for zero, the positions of other points on the scale cannot be compared with respect to relative size. For instance, since the zero point for the temperature scale is arbitrary, it is not correct to say that 64°F is twice as hot as 32°F. This important distinction can be demonstrated with an equivalent example from the centigrade (C) scale. On that scale, 32°F is equal to 0°C and 64°F is equal to about 18°C. Although the distances are identical regardless of the scale used, no one would be likely to say that 18°C was "twice as hot" as 0°C!

The existence of a true zero point is not usually required in order to carry out statistical comparisons, and for analytical purposes, this type of data is often treated in the same fashion as ratio measurement data.

Ratio measurements have all the qualities of nominal, ordinal, and interval measurements. In addition, a true zero point is logically predetermined. This permits comparison of relative size within the data. For example, age is a ratio measure because there is a true point at which aging begins (i.e., birth). Therefore, it is meaningful to say that a six-year-old child is twice as old as a three-year-old.

Evaluation data will usually be a combination of two of the types of above measurements. For example, if the performance of two groups, a treatment group and a control group, is evaluated, the distinction between treatment and control constitutes a nominal measurement. If these groups are given tests that yield ratio measurements, then it would be appropriate to choose a statistical test that is designed for nominal groups with ratio measures.

Although most tests are designed for a specific type of measurement, it is usually possible to drop the distinction between nominal and ordinal and between interval and ratio. When this is done, the former are to be referred to in this text as categorical measurements and the latter as numerical measurements. Figure 8.4 depicts this classification. The possible combinations of types of measurements that are represented by the tests presented later in this chapter include categorical

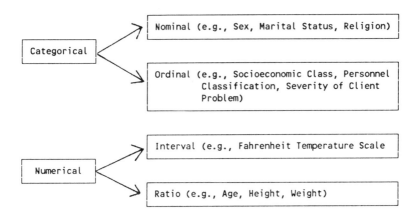

Figure 8.4
Types of Measurements

with numerical, categorical with categorical, and numerical with numerical.

The type of measurement required by a given statistical test is the *minimum* measurement that will work with that test. For example, a test that specifies ordinal data also would work with interval or ratio data, but would not work with nominal data. However, since statistical techniques are fundamentally mathematical, the best choice of test will be the one that uses data from higher levels of measurement. If the data are ordinal, for instance, it may be possible to choose a test specifically for ordinal data that would be more powerful (since it would use the ranking information provided in ordinal data) than a test that specified nominal data.

Another type of measurement distinction has to do with whether the data collected are *paired*. The most common type of paired data in evaluation research is obtained from pretest-posttest designs. Data are considered to be paired whenever one measurement taken can be linked to a second measurement. In the case of pretests and posttests, the measurements are linked when the same study sample takes both the pretest and the posttest (i.e., the score for any particular person on the pretest can be paired up with the score for that same person on the posttest). In contrast, unrelated measurements consist of any two groups of data where there is no meaningful link between the two groups. For instance, the data obtained from a treatment group and a control group would not be paired. (This is a very important distinction in statistics and can be referred to by many labels. The most common terms are paired/not paired, related/unrelated, dependent/independent.) Paired measurements require special statistical tests designed specifically for use with such data.

Type of Distribution

Distribution of the data has to do with how different the scores are and with the ways in which the data vary. For instance, if a parenting skills test is given to 100 clients, it is highly unlikely that all clients will have the same score.

Instead, it is almost certain that the scores will vary. Further, it is often the case that many clients will have scores that are close together, fewer clients will have very high scores, and only a few clients will have very low scores. When the data vary in such a way that most of the scores or measurements tend to fall in the middle of the range of actual scores (i.e., the measurements cluster around the mean) and the frequency of measurements falls off as the distance from the mean increases, the data are considered to have a normal distribution. As shown in Figure 8.5, an idealized graphical representation of this distribution resembles the shape of a bell. For this reason, a normal distribution is often referred to as a bell-shaped curve.

In most cases, the actual data will only approximate a normal distribution. Referring back to Figure 8.1, for example, the distribution tends to have a higher middle, and the frequency of scores becomes lower as the distance from the mean of the data increases. This is a good example of how actual evaluation data might appear. It is not expected that a sample of data will perfectly reflect a normal distribution. In fact, it would be rather strange if it did. The assumption is that, if all members of the population were measured instead of just a sample, the distribution would be perfectly normal. Since the scores only represent a sample, the distribution need only approximate the idealized version.

The concept of a normal distribution is critically important because many statistical tests for numerical measurements assume that the data are normally distributed. If this assumption is violated, the test may be invalid.

- the data collection instrument is a standardized instrument for which documentation regarding validity, reliability, and/or cultural sensitivity is not provided.

Tests for Validity

The validity of an instrument has to do with whether it actually measures what it is purported to measure. There are several ways to judge validity. *Predictive validity* involves comparing the test results with an external criterion. For example, are subjects who score high on a parenting skills test less likely to abuse and neglect their children than those who score low? *Face validity* involves determining whether the instrument captures a commonly agreed upon image of what it is attempting to measure. Tests of face validity include the following methods:

- Ask a group of experts or senior staff to look at the instrument and give an opinion on whether all aspects of a concept (e.g., "good parenting") are being considered.
- Have two different groups that are known to differ on the concept being measured pretest the instrument. For example, a questionnaire measuring stress could be tested on a group that was known to be highly stressed and on another group known to be less stressed. Compare the results of the groups to see if the questionnaire distinguishes between them.

Tests for Reliability

Reliability of an instrument has to do with repeated use. Will results obtained for the same sample be consistent with repeated testing? Reliability is often gauged through the test-retest method. This involves pretesting the instrument twice on the same sample, leaving a time interval of a few days between tests, and checking to see if the scores are similar on both occasions.

Test for Cultural Sensitivity

Cultural sensitivity refers to the appropriateness of the instrument for people from different cultural/ethnic backgrounds. If an instrument is constructed without taking cultural factors into consideration, there may be a systematic bias for some subjects. This sort of effect may be caused by using language that is not interpreted in the same way by different groups. It can also be caused by assumptions that do not hold for some ethnic groups. For example, suppose that an observation instrument called for the observer to rate the "appropriateness" of the physical distance that people kept between themselves during a casual conversation. In fact, the distance that is considered to be polite can vary considerably in different cultures.

Pretest the instrument on all samples that represent ethnic groups of concern to the program. Make sure to include a group that represents the ethnic background(s) of those who designed the instrument. If all groups receive the same scores on the average, then it is likely that each ethnic group regards the concepts being measured in a similar manner. If there are differences in ethnic groups' scores, then either the instrument should be revised to eliminate the biases, or adjustments must be made to interpretations of results, according to the ethnic group being studied.

PRETESTING AND REVISING INSTRUMENTS

If a new instrument has been constructed, or if a standardized instrument has been modified, it will be necessary to pretest the new measure. This procedure applies to all types of instruments, including telephone and face-to-face interview guides, survey questionnaires, audits, observation checklists, and so on. Pretest in this context has a different connotation than when it is used with reference to the research design, as in a "pretest-posttest design." Pretest in the context of instrument construction signifies trial runs of the instrument on various populations for the purpose of uncovering problems and deficiencies that can be corrected before data collection begins.

Pretesting the instrument can be useful in a number of ways. It elicits feedback on the tone, clarity, organization, complexity, and length of the instrument. It can also indicate a preferred format for the documents or a distribution and collection strategy.

A multi-stage pretest and revision process is recommended, regardless of the type of measure to be used. There are four stages in the process: (1) Pretest instrument on staff, colleagues, experts, and so on; (2) revise; (3) pretest instrument using a sample (cases, observations, clients, etc.) that is comparable to the actual study sample; and (4) revise and finalize.

Stage 1: Pretest with Staff, Colleagues, and Experts

Select at least five people to review the instrument. These reviewers should be chosen for their skill, knowledge, and/or other contributions that will enhance the effectiveness of the instrument. It may be appropriate to choose staff members who have not been involved in developing the instrument. The reviewers should include at least one person who is knowledgable about research or instrumentation. It would also be beneficial to have someone who is familiar with the attributes, characteristics, and abilities of the actual sample look over the instrument.

Reviewers should be asked to respond to the instrument as if they were engaged in an actual data collection session (e.g., take the test, fill out the survey, conduct the observation, complete the audit form). They should be instructed to ask questions about anything that is not clear and to make as many comments and recommendations as they deem appropriate in their critique. Their responses to test items, as well as their editorial comments, should be considered in assessing the merits of the instrument. It is also possible to elicit reactions to the instrument by attaching a special questionnaire. General issues that may be pertinent for such a questionnaire are listed in Table 7.13. For in-depth reactions, telephone or personal interviews may be needed.

Stage 2: Revise

Use all of the feedback from all of the Stage 1 pretest sources. Adjust the instrument as needed to correct deficiencies.

Stage 3: Pretest with Comparable Sample

This phase of the pretest process requires locating a sample of clients, cases, or observations that are similar to the actual sample to be used in the study. The pretest sample must *not* have any members in common with the study sample. The reasons for this precaution have to do with distortion of the data. If, for example, some clients were asked to assist in the construction of a survey questionnaire and then later asked to participate in the evaluation by completing the final version of the instrument, it is possible that their answers would be influenced by their prior knowledge of the survey while it was still being designed. This influence may or may not affect the data in ways that would contaminate the results of the study. Therefore, the only way to be

Table 7.13

Instrument Construction Problem Areas

QUESTION CONSTRUCTION

- Vague or ambiguous wording
- Double-barreled questions (two questions in one)
- Double negatives
- Excessively personal questions
- Redundant questions
- Unnecessary or irrelevant questions
- Lengthy or complex questions
- Technical jargon, slang, or unknown expressions
- Uninterpretable or misinterpretable questions
- Threatening wording
- Condescending or insulting questions
- Biased questions

FORMAT

- Crowded/cluttered pages
- Unattractive layout
- Confusing layout
- Overwhelming number of items
- Interspersion of multiple formatting styles

INSTRUCTIONS

- Too few
- Unclear
- Vague
- Too lengthy
- Incomplete

ORGANIZATION

- No order to questions
- Illogical sequence of questions
- Lack of content subsections
- Least important items appear first

LENGTH

- Too time-consuming
- Overwhelming
- Unrealistic, given time allotment

- frequency
- percentage
- range
- mean (average)
- mode
- median

Frequency

A frequency is a figure that represents the number of times that a given event occurred. For example, if a question on a client satisfaction survey requires a yes or no answer, a frequency analysis for that survey item would simply entail a tally of all yes responses and all no responses. The number of yes responses would be the *frequency* of yes responses.

Frequency Distribution: Example 1. Frequencies are commonly reported in graphic form. Figure 8.1, for example, shows how many clients had a given score on a posttest. This representation of the data is called a *frequency distribution* because it shows how the scores are distributed for all the members of the posttest group.

Percentage

A percentage is a frequency that is compared to the total number of responses so that a *proportion* is generated. That proportion is then translated into a percentage by multiplying by 100. For example, if the total number of yes responses to a given survey item was 30 and the total number of all responses was 50, the percentage would be calculated as follows:

$$\frac{\text{Number of Yes Responses}}{\text{Total number of Responses}} \times 100 = \text{Percentage of Yes Responses}$$

$$\frac{30}{50} \times 100 = 60\%$$

Frequency Distribution: Example 2. Using percentages can be a convenient and meaningful strategy. Reporting only that there were 30 yes responses to a question is relatively meaningless, whereas reporting that 60% of the responses were yes conveys the information that over

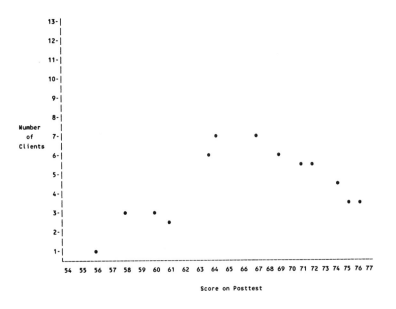

Figure 8.1

Example of a Frequency Distribution for a Posttest Group

half of the responses were positive and specifies exactly the proportion of those responses. In Figure 8.2, there is a sample of a frequency distribution for a rating scale item from a survey; the frequency is presented as a percentage of the entire number of clients.

Range

The range is defined by the highest score and the lowest score obtained in a set of scores. It can be expressed either as the difference between the highest and lowest scores or simply by indicating those two scores. This statistic is useful when the outer boundaries of scores are of interest.

Case Example. A test for knowledge of parenting skills and age-appropriate behaviors was administered to clients who had attended all sessions of the program. The test was designed with 100 items so that

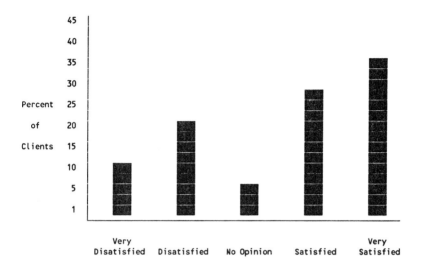

Figure 8.2
Example of a Frequency Distribution for a Survey Item

the lowest possible score was 0 and the highest possible score was 100. When the clients' scores were tabulated, the *range* of scores was 56-76. That is, no client scored less than 56 nor more than 76.

Mean

The mean, also known as the average, is one way to describe a middle value of the data. To generate a mean, it is necessary to specify what is to be averaged (e.g., test scores, the number of hours of attendance at a respite care center, the ratings for a specified survey question, and so on). The data to be averaged are totaled together for all cases, and then divided by the total number of cases. For example, if 20 mothers reported a total of 100 hours attendance at a respite care center, the calculation for the mean number of hours that each mother attended would be calculated as follows:

$$\frac{\text{Total number of response category}}{\text{Total number of respondents / cases}} = \text{Mean}$$

$$\frac{100 \text{ hours}}{20 \text{ mothers}} = 5 \text{ hours mean attendance for each mother}$$

Mode

The mode is the most frequent response in the data. For example, if the number of presentations attended by each of 10 clients were analyzed for the mode, the data might appear as follows:

Client #	Number of Presentations Attended	
A	1	
B	1	Mode = 4
F	2	
H	3	
E	3	Median = 3.5
C	4	
J	4	
D	4	
I	4	
G	5	

Median

The median is the point at which 50% of respondents (or cases) have a higher score and 50% of respondents have a lower score. It is calculated by taking the following steps:

1. Arrange responses (or scores) in numerical order.
2. If there is an even number of responses, add the middle two responses and divide by two.
3. If there is an odd number of responses, the median is the middle score.

In the above sample data for calculation of the mode, for example, the median is: $\frac{3 + 4}{2} = 3.5$.

Case Example. Staff at a primary prevention educational program wanted to evaluate parents' knowledge of child abuse prevention concepts. They wanted to compare the scores of parents for whom their training was the first formal exposure to the material with three sets of parents: parents attending the training who had received previous training; parents who were not attending the training but had received previous training; and parents who were not attending the meeting and had no previous training. All 73 parents of children at one site received a brief self-administered quiz on the reverse of their permission slip, authorizing the school to administer child abuse prevention training to certain that the data will not be distorted by prior knowledge of the instrument is to eliminate from the study sample any member of the pretest sample.

As with the first pretest, this pretest should be conducted as if it were the actual test situation. Simulation of the real test situation will vary according to the type of instrument being pretested.

Survey and Testing Instruments

If the instrument is pretested on clients, create as realistic a testing environment as possible. Do, however, urge respondents to ask for clarification of anything about the instrument that they don't understand (e.g., items, instructions). Note anything that the respondents consistently question, as well as incorrect or unintended uses of the form. If the instrument being pretested is an interview guide, conduct 10 to 30 interviews.

Audit Instrument

An effective way to pretest an audit instrument is to have someone who is not familiar with the measure apply the instrument to a sample of cases. These cases should be similar to those that will be selected for the actual sample. The person pretesting the audit instrument should complete the audit as if it were the actual data collection period. Any difficulties with the measure should be noted. Also, an analysis of the "data" collected during this pretest should be conducted as if they were the actual data. Note any incorrect or unintended uses of the form. Interview the data collector for more information. The guidelines to problem areas shown in Table 7.13 may be used to structure the interview.

Direct Observation Instrument

To pretest an observation instrument, have someone who is not familiar with the instrument use it to document observations of a session that is similar in nature to those that will be observed during the actual study. The observer should note any problems with use of the instrument. Analyze responses on the form for incorrect or unintended uses. Interview the observer for further information, using the guidelines listed in Table 7.13 where needed.

Trouble Spots

Analysis of pretest responses to the instrument should permit detection of consistent errors or other flaws. Typical problems include:

- blank answers,
- unfinished form,
- multiple responses when one response is desired,
- single responses when multiple responses are requested,
- items overlooked,
- misinterpreted items,
- misplaced responses,
- patterned responses, and
- hurried responses.

Problems with the data may not indicate the source of the confusion (e.g., Did the person skip that question on the survey because it was too personal, too unclear, too difficult, or because it was not set out clearly enough on the page?) It may be necessary to conduct follow-up interviews with the pretest respondents to establish the causes of any problems.

Stage 4: Revise and Finalize the Instrument

After the pretest has been completed, each item on the instrument should be carefully scrutinized and all problems noted. Identify the nature of any difficulties; decide whether to rephrase a troublesome item, to delete it, or to adjust it to eliminate the problem. Give final consideration to the overall adequacy of the instrument (e.g., length, format, organization, instructions), and determine if there are any problems along these lines. If so, modify the instrument accordingly. Frequently, decisions about the final form of the instrument warrant group participation at the agency, depending upon the prior involvement of members of the staff.

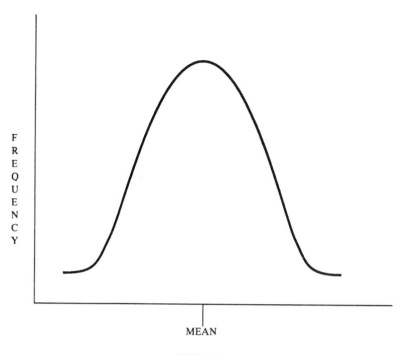

Table 8.5
Normal Distribution

Level of Statistical Significance

One of the most important concepts in inferential statistics is that of *statistical significance*. Statistical comparisons between groups are based fundamentally on *probability*. For instance, how likely is it that the difference in performance between two groups could have occurred by chance? When the appropriate test has been carried out, the resulting level of statistical significance is a measure of the likelihood that scores from two or more groups are truly equal.

Statistical significance is represented as a percentage. If a test were carried out to compare the performance of two different groups on the same test, for example, and the statistical significance were found to be 0.05, that would mean that there was a 5% chance that the performance of both groups was really the same, and that any variations in their scores were due to chance. If, however, there is only a 5% chance that the groups are truly equal, then the groups probably are *not* equal.

In the social sciences, it is conventional to use a statistical significance level of 0.05 as a cut-off point when making decisions about the data. It is common practice for researchers to assume that data that result in a level of statistical significance of 0.05 or less are truly different, and that data that result in a level of significance that is greater than 0.05 (e.g., 0.10) are not truly different. This use of 0.05 as a cut-off, however, is arbitrary and may be altered according to the needs of the researcher.

If it is necessary to be extremely cautious about making claims that there really are differences between the groups, then a researcher may choose to use a smaller level of significance (e.g., 0.01 and 0.02 are also commonly used). This type of caution is prudent in cases where finding a difference between groups when there really is no difference could have serious ethical consequences (e.g., findings that compare the performance of different ethnic, religious, and/or socioeconomic groups). On the other hand, if it would be better to err on the side of finding that a difference exists even if none does, a higher significance level is often chosen, usually 0.10. The appropriate way to use a level of statistical significance is to determine the level that will be used as a cut-off before any tests are carried out.

Assumptions about the Data

Many statistical tests have specific restrictions as to the nature of data that can be used. If those restrictions, called *assumptions* in statistical jargon, are violated, the test may be invalid. In order to use a test, therefore, it is a good idea to ascertain the assumptions and check to see if the data meet them. The minimal requirements for many statistical tests for numerical data are (1) that the data be normally distributed, and (2) that the samples be randomly selected. The assumptions for tests that use categorical data are usually fairly limited; often it is only assumed that the data were gathered from random samples.

Sample Size

In general, statistical tests are very sensitive to the size of the study samples. The larger the sample is, the more likely it is that, if a difference is present in the data, the test will be statistically significant. If, for example, the mean test scores for two groups were 25 and 35 and there were 15 participants in each group, it would be less likely that a significant difference would be found than if there were 50 participants in each group. Further, most of the inferential statistical tests that are used in evaluation research require a minimum number of participants (or cases or responses) in each group. Although the minimum size varies according to the test used, it is a good idea to consider 15 participants in each group to be an absolute minimum when statistical tests will be used. The desirable minimum for most instances is approximately 30 per group. When sample sizes are smaller, it may be necessary to use tests designed specifically for small samples. Such tests are covered later in this chapter in the section on Inferential Statistics for Small Samples.

Statistical Tests for Paired Data

There are several tests for paired data, depending on the type of measurements taken. The following is a list of commonly used tests.

PAIRED T TEST
(CATEGORICAL AND NUMERICAL MEASUREMENTS)

The paired t test compares the difference between the means of two groups of related measures. In evaluation research, this test is used for comparisons of pretest and posttest measures when one sample and the one data collection instrument are used for both the pretest and the posttest.

CASE EXAMPLE

A primary prevention agency wants to conduct an outcome evaluation of its elementary school child abuse prevention program. The evaluator decides to see if the program contributed to positive changes in children's knowledge of self-protective behaviors. A group of children receiving the primary prevention service was randomly selected to participate in the evaluation. This group was pretested about a week before the program was presented in the school, using a data collection instrument that yielded ratio measurements. One to two weeks after participating in the program, the children were posttested with the same instrument. A t test for paired measurements was conducted to determine if there was a statistically significant difference between the pretest and posttest scores. The mean score for the pretest was 65% and for the posttest, 69%. The test did not show a significant difference at the 0.05 level. The evaluator interpreted this as a negative result, that is, that the educational program did not appear to have any effect on the children's ability to answer the test items.

McNEMAR TEST (NOMINAL MEASUREMENTS)

The McNemar test is used for data where both variables are nominal categories and the two measures are paired.

CASE EXAMPLE

A primary prevention agency decided to conduct an evaluation of a new film on emotional abuse. Subjects to view the film were randomly selected from the target population. Before viewing the film, they were asked whether they felt they could identify instances of emotional abuse. Next, they were asked to view the film. They were then surveyed again as to whether they thought they could identify instances of emotional abuse. The results were organized into a table.

The original data showed the group evenly split: 50 viewers thought they would not be able to identify emotional abuse and 50 thought that they would before viewing the film. After viewing the film, only 25 viewers still felt they could not reliably identify instances of emotional abuse. Of the original 50 who thought they could identify the abuse, 35 remained positive after the film, and 15 decided that they could not, after all. On the other hand, of the 50 who originally felt they could not identify emotional abuse, only 10 still thought so after viewing the film. The evaluator conducted the McNemar Test to determine whether the pretest distribution of responses was significantly different from the posttest distribution of responses.

AFTER

B E F O R E		Could Identify	Could Not Identify	Pretest Totals
	Could Identify	35	15	50
	Could Not Identify	40	10	50
	Posttest Totals	75	25	100

PEARSON CORRELATION COEFFICIENT (NUMERICAL DATA)

Correlations have to do with the strength of the relationship between groups of data. That is, are the two groups of data connected in such a way that knowing the value of a piece of data from the first group of data permits a prediction about the second group of data? For example, there is a correlation between the amount of coffee used to make a pot of coffee and the resulting strength of the coffee. If the quantity of coffee beans is known, the strength can be predicted. Similarly, if the strength is known, the quantity of coffee beans can be estimated. This is an example of a *positive* correlation because, as the number of coffee beans increases, so does the strength of the coffee.

Perfect correlations are those that, knowing a given value of the first variable, will predict precisely the value of the second. Perfect correlations do not arise in the real world of evaluation research because any given value of one variable may be influenced by numerous factors. For instance, in a therapeutic program, the correlation between number of staff hours worked and number of clients served is mitigated by factors such as (1) some clients requiring more time and attention than others, (2) some staff being more efficient than others or some staff being more thorough than others, and (3) some programs not being seriously affected by the inclusion of a new client (e.g., a new family member joins an ongoing family therapy session).

One often misunderstood aspect of statistical tests for correlation is that the results of such tests do not address the issue of a cause-and-effect relationship between the variables.

CASE EXAMPLE

An agency providing therapeutic services to children who had been sexually assaulted in the home decided to evaluate the program in terms of the self-esteem of the children. The staff believed that the longer the child spent in the program the higher the level of self-esteem would be. A correlation study was conducted, measuring self-esteem at monthly intervals for a period of six months. All new children entering the program were selected to participate. After six months the two variables, length of time in the program and level of self-esteem, were analyzed. As expected, the results indicated a strong correlation of .47 that was statistically significant at the 0.05 level. However, the evaluator was not able to conclude that the longer time in the program caused the higher levels of self-esteem because several other factors may have been operating; for example, removal from the abusive situation at home may have been an important factor. Additionally, the study did not provide for a follow-up of children who did not continue with the program for the full six months. It may have been that only children whose self-esteem was already beginning to grow were able or willing to continue in the program. The list of alternative explanations is very long. The point is that there is no way to determine causality from a correlational analysis. Perhaps the program was responsible for the increase in self-esteem; perhaps a safer living environment and/or the length of time the child was able to remain in the program were responsible for an increase in self-esteem; perhaps some characteristic intrinsic to some children allowed them to remain in the program. All that is obtained from a correlational analysis is information about the strength of the relationship between the variables, not why or how they are related.

The reasons for using statistical tests in self-evaluation research to examine a correlation include (1) to find out how strong a correlation is between two variables, and (2) to find out if the strength of the correlation is statistically significant.

The results of a test for correlation are presented as a range of values from 0.0 to 1.0, where 0.0 represents no correlation and 1.0 represents perfect correlation. In addition, a level of statistical significance is also calculated.

Sometimes the evaluator will need to examine more than two variables. This is especially true when it is thought that several different factors will influence the value of a given variable (e.g., self-esteem may be influenced by a therapist's efforts but will also be influenced by family attitudes, successful attempts to negotiate school or work, social situations, health, and so on). In situations where more than two variables need to be assessed for correlation, more complex statistics, such as multiple regression techniques, should be used.

SPEARMAN RANK CORRELATION COEFFICIENT
(ORDINAL MEASUREMENTS)

The Spearman Rank Correlation test is very similar to the Pearson Correlation test. The major difference is that it is designed specifically for ordinal data. This test can also be used for interval or ratio data, but it is advisable to use it for interval or ratio data only if the data are from nonnormal distributions.

CASE EXAMPLE

An agency providing therapeutic services to dysfunctional families decided to conduct a correlational study to see if there was a relationship between degree of appropriateness of parental discipline strategies and communication skills. Mothers were chosen as the study population. Families were selected to participate in the study on a random basis as they entered the program. The therapist who worked with a selected family assessed the appropriateness of discipline strategies using a four-point scale after six sessions with the family. The scale consisted of the following categories: very inappropriate, somewhat inappropriate, somewhat appropriate, and very appropriate. An independent observer observed a minimum of two of the six sessions and rated the mother for level of communicative skill on a five point scale: noncommunicative, minimally communicative, somewhat communicative, moderately communicative, and effectively communicative. The evaluator took the communication and discipline ratings for each mother and conducted a Spearman Rank Correlation test to determine the relationship, if any, between the two variables.

Statistical Tests for Unpaired Data

Tests for unpaired data typically involve comparisons between treatment and control groups, and between two (or more) treatment groups.

When more than two groups are to be compared and the variables are categorical (e.g., treatment group A and treatment group B) and numerical (e.g., test scores), the One-Way Analysis of Variance test is appropriate. If the variables are categorical and ordinal (e.g., rating scale), the Kruskal-Wallis One-Way Analysis of Variance is the logical choice. Both of these tests are fairly complex and are beyond the scope of this discussion. The tests described below should be used for comparisons of two groups, unless explicitly stated otherwise.

T TEST (CATEGORICAL AND NUMERICAL DATA)

The t test is one of the most commonly used tests in evaluation research. The calculations are relatively straightforward and the result is given as a level of statistical significance. The standard situation for use of this test is the comparison of two unrelated groups, such as a control group and a treatment group. The scores or responses obtained from the groups must be interval- or ratio-level measurements, such as test scores.

CASE EXAMPLE

An agency needed to do an evaluation of different styles of program delivery. Evaluation participants were randomly selected from the study population and randomly assigned to experience either program delivery style A or program delivery style B. The effectiveness of the different styles was determined by testing participants for knowledge of the content of the program after they had completed it. A t test for unrelated groups was used to compare test scores for the two groups. The mean test score for the group receiving style A was 60% correct. The mean test score for the group receiving style B was 50% correct. The t test showed the two group means to be different; the statistical significance was less than 0.05. The evaluator concluded that style A was more effective.

MANN-WHITNEY U TEST

This test is essentially like the t test, but it is designed specifically for ordinal data.

CASE EXAMPLE

An evaluation was done to compare the results of a parenting skills program for two groups: (1) members of the study sample who had participated in the program (i.e., treatment group), and (2) members of the study sample who were on the waiting list for the program (i.e., control group). The variable measured was type of discipline strategies used by the participants. After the treatment group had completed the program and before the comparison group began the program, the parenting skills for both groups were observed and rated on a five point scale: (1) excellent, (2) good, (3) neutral, (4) poor, and (5) very poor. After the treatment group had completed the program and before the comparison group began the program, the parenting skills for both groups were observed and rated. A Mann-Whitney U test was used to compare the ratings for the two groups. The statistical significance for the difference between the two groups was less than 0.05. The direction of the difference was in favor of the parents who had participated in the program. The evaluator concluded that the program contributed to the more appropriate parenting behaviors of the treatment group.

CHI-SQUARE TEST FOR INDEPENDENCE
(NOMINAL MEASUREMENTS)

The chi-square test for independence compares the distribution of nominal data from two or more groups.

CASE EXAMPLE

A family services agency was considering adopting a new program presentation for parents. There was some concern, however, as to whether the presentation would be equally favorable to both fathers and mothers. As part of an evaluation of the new presentation, a random sample of parents in the study population was selected to view it. After viewing the presentation, the fathers and mothers were asked to rate the program. The results are shown below.

RESPONSE / PARENTS	FAVORABLE	UNFAVORABLE
MOTHERS	30	20
FATHERS	15	35

A chi-square test for independence was conducted to see if there was a significant difference between the distributions of the two groups, mothers and fathers. A finding of a statistically significant difference would mean, in this case, that fathers really were less favorable toward the new presentation than mothers.

Inferential Statistics for Small Samples

Self-evaluation of child abuse prevention services often involves the need to work with small samples of data — samples that are too small for most statistical techniques. In general, the strategy used when samples are too small to use tests such as the t test or chi-square test is to use tests that calculate exact probabilities instead of levels of statistical significance. This means that, rather than obtaining a value that is less than or greater than the level of significance that the evaluator has chosen, these tests will simply produce the actual probability that the data being examined are truly equal.

The three tests discussed in this section vary with respect to the relationship that may hold between variables (e.g., paired or unrelated), but all three will handle any type of measurement, from nominal to ratio. In the event of measurements more sophisticated than nominal, however, it will be necessary to reduce the data to nominal categories before using the tests.

In addition to these tests, note that some statistics software programs will also conduct exact probabilities when other tests are run on samples that turn out to be too small. For example, the statistical software package SPSS[x] (Norusis, 1983) will automatically compute an exact probability using the Fisher exact test (see below) when running a chi-square test of independence if the sample size is less than 20.

BINOMIAL TEST (NOMINAL MEASUREMENT)

The binomial test can only handle one variable with two categories. Thus, for example, mothers in a respite care program might be surveyed about which type of assistance they prefer: one hour a day for three days a week or one block of three hours on one afternoon each week. The single variable is *mothers* and the two categories are *one hour a day* or *three-hour blocks*.